Bond
No.1 for exam success

How To Do
Maths and Non-verbal Reasoning

CEM
(Durham University)

OXFORD
UNIVERSITY PRESS

Great Clarendon Street, Oxford, OX2 6DP, United Kingdom

Oxford University Press is a department of the University of Oxford. It furthers the University's objective of excellence in research, scholarship, and education by publishing worldwide. Oxford is a registered trade mark of Oxford University Press in the UK and in certain other countries

British Library Cataloguing in Publication Data

Data available

978-0-1927-4289-6

10 9 8

Paper used in the production of this book is a natural, recyclable product made from wood grown in sustainable forests. The manufacturing process conforms to the environmental regulations of the country of origin.

Printed in China

Acknowledgements

Page make-up by Oxford Designers & Illustrators

Cover illustrations: Lo Cole

Contents

Standard 11⁺ Maths and
Non-verbal Reasoning Test
(Central pull-out section)

Introduction

The CEM test is a different style to the GL Assessment tests that have been used in the 11+ selective examinations. The test has been created to be 'tutor-proof' in order to create a fairer system for children sitting their entrance exams for many grammar and independent secondary schools. The maths element of the exam will be recognisable from the curriculum your child will have covered in school, but non-verbal reasoning is not a curriculum subject.

What is the CEM Exam?

Since the late 1990s, the Centre for Evaluation and Monitoring, as part of Durham University, has become a leading provider of 11+ assessment. It aims to provide fair assessments and accurate testing to identify those children who are more academically capable. They aim to provide an ever-changing exam format with timed sections covering a mixture of English, verbal reasoning, maths and non-verbal reasoning. In our experience we have found that there are often two exams, which are sat on the same day and each last for 45 minutes with 15 minutes of preparation. Each test is divided into sections that are explained through an audio soundtrack. By creating changeable sections, unpredictable question types, time pressure and high vocabulary levels, CEM does provide an alternative to other 11+ exams.

So is the CEM test 'tutor-proof'?

No book can tell you exactly what will be on the CEM examination paper so it is not possible for any book to teach your child how to jump through an exam hoop. With Bond, we don't believe in simply jumping through exam hoops, as we have spent over 50 years producing quality books and resources that teach children real skills and give them the knowledge and confidence to succeed in any exam. Bond welcomes the emphasis on holistic education and supporting school-based learning.

The skills and techniques needed for the CEM exam are the skills and techniques that underpin this range of books and papers. By following the books, test papers and this *How To Do* guide, your child will have a range of knowledge and skills to help answer any maths and non-verbal reasoning questions. Although there is no guarantee that these question types will come up on every paper, or indeed on any paper, this book provides a solid foundation and covers a broad spectrum of knowledge and question types. In summary, this book will provide a vital resource for all children preparing for the CEM 11+ exam.

Is the CEM paper standard format or multiple-choice?

At the time of writing, it was not possible to confirm what format the CEM exams will take for any specific school, but from the experience of pupils who have already sat the paper, it would appear that there may be elements of both formats. It is usually easier for an exam board to offer multiple choice as papers can then be marked by computer. Note though that a child who can do well in standard format tends to find the multiple-choice paper easier, whereas a child who has only covered a multiple-choice format will find the standard format significantly harder.

Bond prefers to use standard format books with a choice of standard and multiple-choice exam papers. This is to ensure that children have solid skills and techniques under their belt rather than an over-reliance on multiple-choice format skills. The CEM board are keen to stress their desire to mix the questions up and so the Bond CEM style books aim to encourage a child to think of how the same information could be presented in different ways. This is to encourage the logical skills required to deal with any question type that comes up on an exam paper.

What skills does this book cover?

This book will provide guidance, worked examples, practice exercises and top tips in a wide range of maths and non-verbal reasoning areas. These areas are not exhaustive and there are elements of maths and non-verbal reasoning that can belong to more than one area. The topics chosen have been selected to give a logical progression through the book and to ensure all major areas are covered. There are two sections, one covering a wide range of maths skills and the other covering the core elements of non-verbal reasoning.

How is this book organised?

Each section focuses on a particular element or topic in maths, or question type in non-verbal reasoning. The sections are then further divided into subsections where it is helpful to help identify specific strands within an element, for example Factors within the section on Number, or Area within the section on Shape and space.

Key maths areas

- **Number – the core of maths**
  Essential knowledge and understanding of the four operations, place value, decimals and fractions, percentages and ratios.

- **Shape and space**
  Names and properties of 2-D and 3-D shapes; angles; calculation of perimeters, areas and volumes; symmetry.

- **Measure**
  Knowledge of units and methods for carrying out calculations using length, mass, capacity, time, speed and temperature.

- **Algebra**
  Using letters in calculations, solving equations and working out substitutions.

- **Sequences**
  Identifying patterns and connections between terms in a sequence of numbers.

- **Problem solving**
  Looking at methods and strategies for solving problems with more than one step.

- **Data and graphs**
  Covering all types of tables, charts, graphs and data, and how to interpret them.

Key non-verbal reasoning question types

- **Similarities**

  Questions requiring deduction of common features of two or more shapes, and then either application of that to identify another shape which belongs, or identification of the odd one out.

- **Analogies**

  Deduction of the relationship or connection between a pair of shapes, which is then applied to find the pattern that will complete the second pair in the same way.

- **Sequences and grids**

  Identifying the links between a series of shapes or patterns and applying that to find the next or missing one, including both linear patterns and patterns in a grid.

- **Codes**

  Working out a code from a given set of shapes and codes in order to find the code for an uncoded shape or pattern.

- **Reflections and Rotations**

  Careful observation of a series of shapes or patterns to find the one that is a reflection or rotation of the first given shape.

- **Cubes**

  Linking nets of cubes with the 3-D images of a cube.

Within all of these question types there are a number of variables that have to be considered, and to solve any question these have to be identified. They relate to:
- shape or shapes involved
- position which may include angle
- number
- pattern or shading
- size.

Each section is labelled to match the tutorial links which can be found throughout the Bond CEM Maths and Non-verbal Reasoning Assessment Papers to give a clear structure to both this book and the assessment papers. Each question type is introduced and a worked example is given, followed by questions for your child to work through to ensure there is a thorough understanding of each question type. There are many examples of each question style for a child to try, with a clear progression through the book based on understanding techniques before moving on to the next section. In the assessment papers, these individual skills are mixed throughout each paper to replicate an exam. This is an excellent way of consolidating skills as they are understood and recalled in each paper. If a child is struggling with the assessment papers, it is easy to then refer back to this book for further consolidation of any tricky areas.

In the centre of the book there is then a full examination paper testing each of the question types covered in the book. This book also includes a 'How do you prepare for the exam?' section to help with the actual exam itself, how to deal with timing issues and how to deal with questions that your child may have never seen. This is followed by a glossary containing key terms and an answer section so that you can see how you would have scored. Finally, there is a resources section with books and free online materials that will help to support your child.

How can you use this book?

This book is designed for use by children and parents to help prepare for a CEM 11⁺ exam. It includes a range of top tips and suggestions. A wide range of question styles that may be found on the CEM test paper are presented with guidance and worked examples to help answer the questions. This book provides a step-by-step tutorial that can be worked through from start to finish. It will become a reference tool to look up question types that your child might struggle with and worked examples to explain how they are solved. The book covers a wide range of question types that can also complement other exams and will work in conjunction with the range of maths and non-verbal reasoning CEM books and exam papers.

Why use this book?

How To Do CEM Maths and Non-verbal Reasoning is part of the long-established and well-known Bond series. The Bond range has been used for over 50 years and has been trusted by thousands of pupils, parents, teachers and tutors. This heritage provides confidence and a full range of supporting materials and resources.

A key strength with the Bond books is that all of the key skills build up gradually and are consolidated in each paper. Instead of learning one skill and then moving on to another, the Bond books have the same question types in each paper which builds in consolidation. Instead of reaching the end of a book having forgotten the skills learnt, the Bond books keep each skill fresh. In order to learn each technique, this book gives an explanation and then several example questions. There is the opportunity for children to practise each technique, with regular recaps for children to consolidate each technique. The central pull-out test is an ideal way of checking that each technique has been fully understood.

As the CEM exam is not pinned down to a set of question types, it is especially important for a child to have solid knowledge that can be used in a variety of ways. The skills in this book are presented in different formats and the assessment papers that go with this book provide additional practice at each level.

Checklist

What do you need to use with this book?

✔ A ready supply of **pencils** and **erasers**

✔ Plenty of clean **paper** for working out

✔ A quiet, **well-lit area** in which to work

You may also find it useful to have:

• A small plain mirror for help with symmetry work

• Scissors and paper for help with cubes and nets questions

• *Bond How To Do 11⁺ Maths* for further help and explanations.

✔ PARENT TIP

Your exam might be standard format, where a pupil writes the answer on a line, or it might be in multiple-choice format, where a pupil has a choice of answers from which to select. If a child can complete a standard format paper, then a multiple-choice paper is advantageous. If, however, your child only completes multiple-choice papers, a standard format will be significantly harder, so make sure that your child feels secure with all of these question types and can then practise their newfound skills with the CEM Maths and Non-verbal Reasoning Assessment Papers.

CEM How To Do Maths and Non-verbal Reasoning

Parent tips and information

When should you start using this book?

The Parents' Guide to the 11+ is a great resource for assessing your child and for creating your own learning plan. This will suggest the best time to begin with an 11+ programme, but whether your child has a year or a month before the exam, this book should prove useful.

What else can I do to support my child through the 11+?

The 11+ process should be a fun journey of extending your child's love of learning, which they begin from the moment they are born. Fostering observational skills, counting, questioning, problem solving and thinking logically are such important skills that it is never too late, nor too early to begin this process. Encourage your child to do well at school and offer appropriate support and encouragement with their school homework. Talk about the work they have done in school and reinforce number skills during everyday tasks and conversations.

Although it is wonderful to give your child the experience of museums, galleries, cultural events and travel, much effective learning costs very little. From baking, gardening and various hobbies through to jigsaw puzzles, sudoku and word searchers, there are many activities that can be done easily at home which will support the development of number logic, reasoning and the development of mathematical ideas. A balance of different activities makes the whole learning process more enjoyable for your child and is more effective than a single focus or occasional event.

In terms of extending maths and non-verbal reasoning, the following are some ideas that you can take on board to help your child to develop knowledge and skills:

- Around the house, ask questions ranging from simple 'How many glasses do we need?' when setting the table, through to 'How much water do I need to add?' from a set of instructions
- Ask your child to look up times of television programmes, bus timetables and journey distances and talk about their duration
- Go shopping and encourage your child to read signs and labels, for example working out which offer is the best value
- Play with words and numbers with games such as Scrabble®, Boggle® and Triolet®
- Develop spatial awareness and improve memory through games such as Pelmanism
- Improve observational skills and shape awareness by doing jigsaw puzzles
- Use card games such as Play2Pass® to sharpen non-verbal observational skills
- Apply number logic with puzzles such as sudoku.

Don't underestimate the power of 'fun' learning:
- watch quiz programmes on television
- watch science and discovery programmes
- play board games that extend vocabulary and general knowledge
- take part in quizzes
- do crosswords together
- turn number plates into sums to work out.

1 Number

(A) Types of numbers

Decimal numbers	Numbers in our base 10 system, but commonly used to refer to those numbers when they are written with a decimal point, for example 103.4, 7.25
Cardinal numbers	First (1st), second (2nd) *or half*, third (3rd), fourth (4th) *or quarter*, fifth (5th), sixth (6th) and so on.
	Used to refer to order, position, dates or fractions
Even numbers	Whole numbers that are divisible exactly by 2
Odd numbers	Whole numbers that are not divisible exactly by 2
Roman numerals	Numbers written using I, V, X, L, C, D, M
	I = 1, V = 5, X = 10, L = 50, C = 100, D = 500, M = 1000
Prime numbers	Numbers that can only be divided exactly by 1 and the number itself
	The first ten prime numbers are 2, 3, 5, 7, 11, 13, 17, 19, 23, 29.
Triangular numbers	Numbers of dots that can be placed to form a triangle with each row increasing by one

    •   For example 1, 3, 6, 10

    •   •

    •   •   •

    •   •   •   •

Square numbers	Numbers made by multiplying a number by itself
	$2 \times 2 = 4$ can be written as 2^2
	The first ten square numbers are 1, 4, 9, 16, 25, 36, 49, 64, 81, 100.
	The number that has been multiplied by itself to give the square number is called the square root of that number. For example, 2 is the square root of 4, and 5 is the square root of 25.

Cube numbers	Numbers made by multiplying a number by itself two times

$2 \times 2 \times 2 = 8$ can be written as 2^3

The first five cube numbers are 1, 8, 27, 64, 125.

The number that has been multiplied by itself twice to give the cube number is called the cube root of that number. For example, 2 is the cube root of 8, and 5 is the cube root of 125.

(B) Addition and subtraction

Instant recognition and recall of number bonds will make your mental addition and subtraction fast and accurate – essential for the Short Maths questions on CEM papers and mental maths tests, so play lots of number games!

 PARENT TIP

On car journeys play 'Make a 100' with one player saying a number less than 100, and the other player responding quickly with the number that makes it up to 100.

Short maths questions are usually written in digits, so look carefully at how the question is written to decide whether you need to add or subtract the numbers.

Note: The same calculation can be written in many different ways!

Worked example

$365 + ? = 500$ *How many must be added on to 365 to make 500?*

$500 - 365 = ?$ *Taking away 365 from 500 leaves how many?*

$500 - ? = 365$ *How many must be taken away from 500 to leave 365?*

These all require you to find the difference between 365 and 500.

Either find the difference by counting on:

365 to 370	**5**
370 to 400	**30**
400 to 500	**100**
Total	**135**

Or set out as a block calculation:

$$\begin{array}{ccc} {}^4 5 & {}^1 0^9 & {}^1 0 \\ - \quad 3 & 6 & 5 \\ \hline 1 & 3 & 5 \end{array}$$

In longer maths questions or word problems, read the question carefully, looking for the words that tell you what operation you need to do.

Checklist

✓ These are all terms for adding: add, sum, total, altogether, plus, increase, more, combine

✓ These are all terms for subtracting: subtract, take away, difference, decrease, deduct, remove, how much more than, how much less than, reduce

 **PARENT TIP**

You can play a quick game using two dice. Both players start with 100 points and take turns to throw the two dice. Add the two numbers together and subtract from 100. Answers have to be called out and can be challenged by the other player! The first player to get down to zero is the winner.

Now it's your turn!

Fill in the missing numbers. (6)

1 46 + 28 + _____ = 100

2 489 + 241 = _____

3 835 − 345 = _____

4 416 − _____ = 328

5 _____ + 39 = 205

6 _____ − 271 = 268

7 Tim spends £1.46 on fruit, £1.14 on a loaf of bread and 80p on a comic. (1)
What is the total cost? _____

8 Sonia has a £20 note. She buys a book for £12.99. How much does she (1)
have left? _____

C *Multiplication and division*

Multiplication and division are the converse of each other, so once you know your times tables well you will be able to tackle both types of operation with confidence.

Learn your times tables from × 2 to × 12 and practise often!

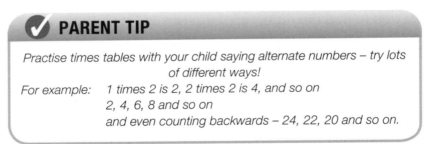 **PARENT TIP**

Practise times tables with your child saying alternate numbers – try lots of different ways!

For example: 1 times 2 is 2, 2 times 2 is 4, and so on
2, 4, 6, 8 and so on
and even counting backwards – 24, 22, 20 and so on.

When tackling problems that require long multiplication or long division, make sure you estimate the answer first. Round the numbers so that the calculation can be done in your head and then check your answer against the estimate.

Which of these answers would be the most reasonable estimate for these calculations?

329 × 17 =   3000   6000   600   9000

89,728 ÷ 49 =   190   2000   1400   800

If you find these tricky, look up Rounding in section 1H for more help and practice.

$586 \times 23 = ?$ Round both numbers to give 600×20, which is $600 \times 10 \times 2$

so our estimate is $600 \times 10 \times 2 = 6000 \times 2 = 12{,}000$

Work out the answer in your head by breaking down into chunks and then adding each chunk together:

586×3 is 1758 → 586×20 is $11{,}720$ → $11720 + 1758$ is **13,478**

Check with estimate: Is the answer approximately 12,000?   Yes

Or use a block calculation:

		5	8	6
		$\times$	2	3
1	1_1	7_1	2	0
	1	7_2	5_1	8
1	$\mathbf{3_1}$	**4**	**7**	**8**

Worked example

$3150 \div 45 = ?$ Round both numbers to give $3000 \div 50$, so the estimate is 60.

To work out the answer:

Either: Break down the divisor into factor pairs: 5×9

Then divide the calculation by each number in turn:

$3150 \div 5$ is 630 → $630 \div 9 = 70$
Check with estimate: Is this approximtely 60? Yes
So answer is **70**

Or: Set out the multiples of 45

45,	90,	135,	180,	225,	270,	**315,**	360
1	2	3	4	5	6	7	8

By doing this, you identify that 45 goes exactly into 315 seven times

so it goes **70** times into 3150.

What to do if there is a remainder

In a question where the number cannot be divided exactly, look carefully at what is being asked for, as this will tell you how you need to express the remainder. Remember that the CEM test papers will use a wide variety of question types so you must always read the question very carefully.

Here are four different examples using the same numbers:

Worked examples

1 A party of 240 people are going on a coach trip. If each coach can take 32 people, *how many coaches* will be needed?

   32 is $8 \times 4 \longrightarrow 240 \div 8 = 30 \longrightarrow 30 \div 4 = 7$ with a remainder of 2, so 8 coaches will be needed

2 An amount of £240 is shared between a class of 32 children. *How much will they each get*?

   As it is money, introduce the decimal point and two decimal places for the pence.

   32 is 8×4, so
   £240.00 $\div 8 = 30.00 \longrightarrow 30.00 \div 4 = 7.50 \longrightarrow$ They will each get **£7.50**

3 Work out $240 \div 32$ giving your answer as a *mixed number*.

   32 is 8×4, so $\quad 240 \div 8 = 30 \longrightarrow 30 \div 4 = 7$ R2, which is $\frac{2}{4}$ or $\frac{1}{2}$,

   so answer as a mixed number is $7\frac{1}{2}$

4 A group of 240 people arrive to take part in a competition. If 32 teams can take part, *how many people* will not be able to take part?

   32 is 8×4, so $\quad 240 \div 8 = 30 \longrightarrow 30 \div 4 = 7.5$ teams.
   Half a team is 16 people, so **16 people cannot take part.**

So… read the question carefully!

Order of operations

When you have a calculation with a mixture of multiplication, division, addition and subtraction, brackets may be used around the part of the calculation that needs to be worked out first. After the brackets, work out any terms using indices (see Section 1F), then work from left to right, doing any division and multiplication operations before carrying out any additions or subtractions.

Worked examples

$4 \times (3 + 5) - (4 + 3^2) = 4 \times 8 - (4 + 9) = 32 - 13 = \mathbf{19}$

Brackets and indices   multiplication then subtraction

If the calculation is written like this: $7 \times 3 + 5 \times 10 \div 2 - 11 =$

To work out the order of operations it can help to add brackets:

$(7 \times 3) + (5 \times 10 \div 2) - 11 = 21 + 25 - 11 = \mathbf{35}$

Brackets

When a series of operations are listed altogether in one calculation, then brackets may be used. They identify which sections need to be worked out first. You will also come across them in algebra and equations (see section 4).

So in this example, work out what is in the brackets first:

Worked example

$(35 + 77) - (14 \times 2)$ which gives $112 - 28 = 84$

Having carried out any operations in brackets, complete the calculation by working from left to right. Remember that any multiplication or division operations are done before any additions or subtractions.

In this calculation, brackets first
$$35 + 5 - 24 + 3 \times 5 + (10 + 2) = 35 + 5 - 24 + 3 \times 5 + 12$$

Multiplication next
$$35 + 5 - 24 + 3 \times 5 + 12 = 35 + 5 - 24 + 15 + 12$$

Then complete working left to right $\longrightarrow$
$$35 + 5 - 24 + 15 + 12 = \mathbf{43}$$

We have not yet mentioned indices (see section 1F) but note here that they would be worked out after any brackets and before the multiplication and division operations.

The mnemonic **BIDMAS** can help you to remember the order:

Brackets first

Indices next

Division and **M**ultiplication in order from left to right

Addition and **S**ubtraction elements again working from left to right

---

Now it's your turn!

9 85.2 ÷ 6 = _____ (5)

10 47 × 14 = _____

11 35 × _____ = 385

12 6020 ÷ _____ = 1505

13 Share £49.50 equally between 3 children. _____

14 Party bags have 28 poppers in each bag. (1)
   a How many bags needed for each child in a school of 217 to have one
      popper each? _____
   b How many are left over? _____

15 If 1.4 million people across 8 states watch a special match on TV, on
    average how many in each state are watching? _____ (1)

16 $17 - 3 \times 2 + (4^2 - 3) \times 5 =$ _____ (1)

D Multiples

When two whole numbers are multiplied together, the answer is a multiple of
both numbers.

For example: 48 is a multiple of 4 and 12 (4 × 12) and 15 is a multiple of 3 and 5 (3 × 5)

As you recite your times tables, each number or answer is a multiple.

Now it's your turn!

17–20 Complete these strings of multiples using your knowldge of the 3, 4, 7 (4)
and 9 times tables.

Multiples of 3	3	6	9	12							
Multiples of 4	4	8	12								
Multiples of 7	7	14									
Multiples of 9	9										

From the table, you can see that 12 is a multiple of both 3 and 4, that is, it is a
common multiple.

PARENT TIP

*Speed completion of multiplication
grids is an excellent way to consolidate
knowledge of times tables.*

REMEMBER!

Short maths questions often ask you to
identify common multiples, and spotting
common multiples quickly can help solve
longer maths problems.

✓ PARENT TIP

When out in the car look at car number plates, spotting numbers which are multiples of 3, 5 etc.

Ⓔ Factors

The answer resulting from multiplying whole numbers together is called the product of those numbers, and the numbers themselves are factors of that product. When the times tables are learnt in a '2 times 3 is 6' format, then the first two numbers, 2 and 3 in this example, are factors of the product, in this case 6.

Checklist

✓ A number that can divide into another, larger number an exact number of times is a **factor** of the larger number.

✓ Every whole number can be divided exactly by both 1 and itself, so all whole numbers have at least two factors.

✓ If a whole number can *only* be divided exactly by 1 and itself, it is a **prime** number.

Secure knowledge of your times tables will help you to identify factors very quickly.

Short maths questions may ask you to identify factors of one or more numbers, or to list the pairs of factors.

REMEMBER!

A pair of factors for any number is a pair of numbers, which when multiplied together give the original larger number.

Here are some quick ways to identify factors:

● 2 is always a factor of even numbers
  Just look at the last digit to identify an even number!
  – If, having divided the given number by 2 you still have an even number, it can be divided by 2 again, making 2×2, which means that 4 is a factor of the original number.

  – If, having divided the given number by 2 twice, you still have an even number, it can be divided by 2 again, making $2 \times 2 \times 2$, which means that 8 is a factor of the original number.

Worked example

What are the factors of 104?   **Factors**

$104 \div 2 \rightarrow 52$ 2

              $52 \div 2 = 26$ 2×2 4

                       $26 \div 2 = 13$ $2 \times 2 \times 2$ 8

Check: $104 \div 4 = 26$

                      Check: $104 \div 8 = 13$

As factors must divide exactly into the given number, they can be written as pairs.

The eight factors of 104, the example above, can be written as four pairs:

104×1 $\qquad$ 52×2 $\qquad$ 26×4 $\qquad$ 13×8

- 3 is a factor of a number if the individual digits of that number add up to a multiple of 3

Worked example

What are the factors of 279?   Factors

$2 + 7 + 9 = 18$, a multiple of 3 $\qquad$ $279 \div 3 = 93$ $\qquad\qquad$ **3**

$9 + 3 = 12$, a multiple of 3 $\qquad\quad$ $93 \div 3 = 31$ $\quad$ 3×3 $\qquad$ **9**

$3 + 1 = 4$, not a multiple of 3 $\qquad$ *Check: $279 \div 9 = 31$*

The six factors of 279, the example above, can be written as three pairs:

279×1 $\qquad$ 93×3 $\qquad$ 31×9

- 5 is a factor of all numbers ending in 0 or 5

Worked example

What are the factors of 275? $\qquad\qquad\qquad\qquad$ Factors

$275 \div 5 = 55$ $\qquad\qquad\qquad\qquad\qquad\qquad\qquad$ **5**

$\qquad\qquad\qquad$ $55 \div 5 = 11$ $\qquad$ 5×5 $\qquad$ **25**

Check: $275 \div 25 = 11$

The six factors of 275, the example above, can be written as three pairs:

275×1 $\qquad$ 55×5 $\qquad$ 11×25

- 6 is a factor of a number if it is an even number and also divisible by 3
- 10 is a factor of all numbers ending in 0

 PARENT TIP

Look at car number plates when you are out walking and spot those which are multiples of 3 or 5.

Now it's your turn!

21 Which of these numbers have 7 as a factor? Underline the answers. (1)

16   14   17   81   72   56   40   35

22 What are the factors of: (4)

a 226 _____

b 165 _____

c 87 _____

d 144 _____

23 Underline the numbers which are prime numbers. (1)

21   13   9   27   31   17

24 Which of these numbers are factors of both 536 and 372? (1)

1   2   3   4   5   6   7   8   9

(F) Squares and cubes

A square number is the product of any whole number multiplied by itself:

For example: $5 \times 5 = 25$, so 25 is a square number and 5 is the square root of 25

If a number is to be squared it is written with a small ^{2}: $5^2 = 5 \times 5 = 25$

The square root of a number is written using this $\sqrt{}$ sign: $\sqrt{25} = 5$

Learn the first 13 square numbers so that you can recognise them immediately in any question:

1   4   9   16   25   36   49   64   81   100   121   144   169

They are called square numbers because if that number of dots is arranged in rows to form an array, a square can be made.

```
•   •   •   •   •
•   •   •   •   •
•   •   •   •   •
•   •   •   •   •
•   •   •   •   •
```

Remember, area uses square units, for example, cm^2 or m^2 (to read more about measuring area see section 2E Area).

A cube number is the product of a number times itself twice, that is, $3 \times 3 \times 3$, so the cube of 3 is 27.

The first six cubic numbers are: 8, 27, 64, 125, 216

Any numbers written as small digits after a term, such as the ^{2} in 3^2 or the ^{3} in y^3, are called indices.

Remember that volume uses cubic units, for example cm^3 or m^3 (to read more about measuring volume see section 2F Volume and capacity).

Now it's your turn!

Underline the odd one out. (2)

25 45   70   95   22   30

26 9   81   60   49   100

27 What is $3^2 + 6^2 + \sqrt{100}$? _____ (1)

28 List five pairs of factors for 48: _____ (1)

29 Complete these number triplets. The first has been done for you. (4)

a 15 / 3 5   **b** 60 / 5 ___   **c** 18 / ___ 6   **d** ___ / 7 6   **e** ___ / 8 3

G Place value

You need to know the value of a digit wherever it appears in a number.

1,000,000		millions
100,000		hundreds of thousands
10,000		tens of thousands
1000		thousands
100		hundreds
10		tens
1		units or ones
	0.1	tenths
	0.01	hundredths
	0.001	thousandths

Now it's your turn!

Check your knowledge of place value by giving the value of each digit in this number. (9)

	2,648,139.57	
	What is the value of this digit in the number above?	Value
30	1	
31	2	
32	3	
33	4	
34	5	
35	6	
36	7	
37	8	
38	9	

Understanding place value is important for ordering and rounding.

When ordering numbers, you start by looking at the number of columns, and then the value of the digits in each column, starting with the highest value column (that is, the column on the left of any number).

Follow the simple steps in this example to see how to order numbers from highest value to lowest value.

REMEMBER!

The longest number is not necessarily the biggest number!

Worked example

Order these numbers from highest to lowest:

a 1,130,947   b 983,000.38   c 938,999

d 347,572.1   e 79,000.78   f 401,329

How many places are there in each number to the left of the decimal point?

a 1,130,947   b 983,000.38   c 938,999

Number of places before
decimal point: 7   6   6

d 347,572.1   e 79,000.78   f 401,329

Number of places before
decimal point: 6   5   6

Option **a** has the greatest number of places to the left of the decimal point and **e** has the fewest. This means that **a** is the greatest number.

To order **b**, **c**, **d** and **f**, which all have the same number of digits to the left of the decimal point, look at the value of the digit in the column furthest on the left, which has been underlined

b 9̲83,000.38   c 9̲38,999   d 3̲47,572.1   f 4̲01,329

We see that it is 9 in **b** and **c**, 3 in **d** and 4 in **f**, so f > d, and **b** and **c** are greater than both of them.

As **b** and **c** have the same number in the hundreds of thousands column, we now need to look at the next column along, which is the tens of thousands:

b 98̲3,000   c 93̲8,999   8 > 3 so **b** > **c**

We can now order all six numbers from greatest to least:

Answer: a 1,130,947 > b 983,000.38 > c 938,999 > f 401,329 >
d 347,572.1 > e 79,000.78

When ranking numbers with decimal points, the same process is followed. As each column from the left is inspected in turn, continue if necessary to the digits in the decimal places, that is the tenths, hundredths and so on.

(H) Rounding

When rounding a number, identify the level of accuracy required by counting the number of places from the decimal point being asked for. If the digit in the column to the right of the one being requested is 4 or less, then the numbers in that column and other spaces up to the decimal point are replaced by zeroes. If the digit in the column to the right of the one being requested is 5 or more, then the numbers in that column and other spaces up to the decimal point are replaced by zeroes *and* the number in the column to the left, that is, the column being requested, is increased by one.

Worked examples

Round 46,385 to the nearest thousand.

The thousands column is the 4th column from the decimal point.

Inspect the digit in the column to the right of that place, that is, the 3rd column.

This is the hundreds column and in this example the digit is 3, so round down.

The digits in the hundreds, tens and units columns are replaced by zeroes, giving an answer of **46,000**.

Round 46,835 to the nearest thousand.

The thousands column is the 4th column from the decimal point.

Inspect the digit in the column to the right of that place, that is, the 3rd column.

This is the hundreds column and in this example the digit is 8, so round up.

The digits in the hundreds, tens and units columns are replaced by zeroes.

As 8 > 5, the number of thousands is increased by 1, from 46 thousand to 47 thousand, giving an answer of **47,000**.

Now it's your turn!

39 What is the value of the 8 in each of these numbers? (4)

    a 78,450 _____   **c** 38.512 _____

    b 395.285 _____   **d** 7,802,746 _____

40 Round these numbers to the nearest whole number. (5)

    a 469.51 _____   **c** 9191.91 _____   **e** 999.67 _____

    b 199.79 _____   **d** 0.0987 _____

41 Order these numbers from highest to lowest. (1)

    783.84   758.66   793.01   739.93   791.34   758.48

_____

① Fractions

A fraction is a part of one whole.

Simple fractions are written as one number over another, for example $\frac{1}{2}$, $\frac{1}{4}$ or $\frac{1}{3}$.

The bottom number of any fraction is called the denominator – it shows how many equal parts the whole has been divided into.

The top number is the numerator – it shows how many of those equal parts are being considered.

For example in $\frac{3}{5}$, 5 is the denominator – the whole has been divided into five equal parts.

3 is the numerator – the number of equal parts being considered.

Where the denominator is 2, the fractions are called halves and where it is 4 they are called quarters.

Other fractions are named using ordinal numbers, for example 3rds (thirds), 5ths (fifths), 8ths (eighths).

There are other types of fractions in addition to simple or common fractions. A fraction with a value greater than 1 – that is, when the numerator is greater than the denominator – is called an improper fraction. Two or more fractions which have the same value, even though they may have different denominators, are called equivalent fractions because they are equal in value.

Checklist

- ✓ **Common fractions** are simple fractions with a whole number for the numerator and a whole number for the denominator, with the numerator being less than the denominator.
- ✓ **Improper fractions** are fractions where the numerator is greater than the denominator, making them 'top heavy'.
- ✓ **Mixed numbers** are numbers made up of whole numbers and fractions, such as $7\frac{1}{2}$.
- ✓ **Equivalent fractions** are fractions with the same value. $\frac{1}{2}$ is the same as $\frac{2}{4}$, so $\frac{1}{2}$ and $\frac{2}{4}$ are equivalent fractions.
- ✓ **Decimal fractions** are numbers with digits after the decimal point indicating tenths, hundredths, and so on.

To change an improper fraction into a mixed number:

1 Divide the denominator into the numerator to find how many wholes can be made.

2 Express the remainder as a fraction.

To change a mixed number into an improper fraction:

1 Multiply the whole number by the denominator.

2 Add on the numerator.

3 Express the answer as a 'top heavy' fraction.

Worked examples

1 Convert the improper fraction $\frac{7}{4}$ to a mixed number.

   $7 \div 4 = 1$ remainder 3; the remainder can be expressed as $\frac{3}{4}$

   Answer $= \mathbf{1\frac{3}{4}}$

2 Convert the mixed number $5\frac{7}{8}$ to an improper fraction.

   $5 \times 8 = 40, \ 40 + 7 = 47$

   Answer is $\frac{47}{8}$

To find a fraction equivalent to another fraction, multiply the numerator and the denominator by the same number.

> **REMEMBER!**
>
> Both the numerator and the denominator must be multiplied by the same number.

Worked example

Give three fractions that are all equivalent to $\frac{3}{5}$:

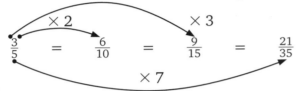

$$\frac{3}{5} \ \overset{\times 2}{=} \ \frac{6}{10} \ \overset{\times 3}{=} \ \frac{9}{15} \ \overset{\times 7}{=} \ \frac{21}{35}$$

To express a fraction in its lowest terms, you divide both the numerator and the denominator by the same number, which must go exactly into both numbers. You repeat this until there are no common factors between the numerator and denominator.

This process is called **simplifying** or **reducing** fractions.

> **REMEMBER!**
>
> Being able to identify factors and multiples of a number quickly makes simplifying fractions much easier!

Worked example

Simplify the following fractions:

$\frac{9}{21}$ $\div$ both by 3 $= \frac{3}{7}$

$\frac{20}{24}$ $\div$ both by 2 $= \frac{10}{12}$ → $\div$ both by 2 $= \frac{5}{6}$

       [or $\div$ both by 4 $= \frac{5}{6}$]

$\frac{16}{40}$ $\div$ both by 2 $= \frac{8}{20}$ → $\div$ both by 2 $= \frac{4}{10}$ → $\div$ both by 2 $= \frac{2}{5}$

       [or $\div$ both by 8 $= \frac{2}{5}$]

To work out any fraction of a given quantity, divide the quantity by the denominator and then multiply the answer by the numerator.

Worked example

What is $\frac{3}{4}$ of 344?

Divide by denominator: $344 \div 4 = 86$

Multiply by numerator: $86 \times 3 = 258$

Answer: 258

To express one number as a fraction of another, write the first number over the second and then simplify as far as possible. Remember to check that both numbers are in the same units.

Worked example

Express 8 cm as a fraction of a metre.

1 m = 100 cm, so the fraction is $\frac{8}{100} = \frac{4}{50}$

$= \frac{2}{25}$

Now it's your turn!

42 Underline the fractions that are equivalent. (1)

$\frac{5}{7}$ $\quad$ $\frac{4}{9}$ $\quad$ $\frac{3}{5}$ $\quad$ $\frac{8}{12}$ $\quad$ $\frac{7}{14}$ $\quad$ $\frac{12}{18}$ $\quad$ $\frac{10}{7}$ $\quad$ $\frac{3}{10}$

43 Reduce these fractions to their lowest terms: (3)

$\quad$ **a** $\frac{32}{48}$ _____ $\frac{2}{3}$ $\quad$ **b** $\frac{14}{20}$ _____ $\frac{7}{10}$ $\quad$ **c** $\frac{64}{80}$ _____ $\frac{4}{5}$

44 What is $\frac{5}{7}$ of 1358? _____ 975 (1)

45 Express 525 g as a fraction of 1 kg _____ $\frac{21}{40}$ (1)

46 If $\frac{1}{3}$ of an amount of money is £32.00, what is the value of $\frac{1}{4}$ of the amount? (1)

£21.50

J Percentages

Percentages are fractions with 100 as the denominator, so 50% is $\frac{50}{100}$, 93% is $\frac{93}{100}$, and so on.

To find the value of a certain percentage of a number, write the percentage as a fraction over 100, then follow the steps set out in section 1I above.

> **Worked example**
>
> What is 70% of £2750?
>
> Remember: 70% is the same as $\frac{70}{100}$
>
> This can be simplified to $\frac{7}{10}$
>
> Then...   Divide by denominator, which is 10:   £2750 ÷ 10 = £275
>
>   Multiply by numerator, which is 7:   £275 × 7 = £1925
>
>   Answer: **£1925**

To express one number as a percentage of another number, make them into a fraction and multiply by 100.

> **Worked example**
>
> Express 38 as a % of 2000.
>
> $$\frac{38}{2000} \times 100 = \frac{3800}{2000}$$
>
> $=$ $\frac{38}{20}$ *(dividing the top and the bottom both by 100)*
>
> $=$ $\frac{19}{10}$ *(dividing the top and the bottom both by 2)*
>
> $=$ **1.9%**   *(dividing the top and the bottom both by 10)*

In many word problems, an amount is often increased or decreased by a certain percentage.

There are two stages to solving these problems:

1 Calculate the percentage.
2 Add or subtract the percentage according to whether it is an increase or decrease.

> **Worked example**
>
> The price of fuel is increased by 3%.
>
> The old price was £1.36 per litre.
>
> What is the new price per litre, rounded to the nearest whole penny?
>
> To find 3% of £1.36:
>
> Either: $\frac{3}{100} \times 136$ *(working in pence)* $= \frac{(3 \times 136)}{100}$
>
> $= \frac{3}{50} \times 68$ *(dividing top and bottom by 2)*
>
> $= \frac{3}{25} \times 34$ *(dividing top and bottom by 2)*
>
> $= \frac{102}{25} = 4\frac{2}{25} = 4.08$
>
> $= 4.08\text{p} = $ **4p** *(rounded to the nearest whole penny)*

Or: 100% is £1.36, which is 136p

So 1% is 1.36p

So 3% is (1.36 × 3)p = 4.08p = **4p** (*rounded to the nearest whole penny*)

New price is original price + the increase = (£1.36 + 4p) per litre

= **£1.40 per litre**

Note: See how easy it is to change fractions to percentages to decimal fractions!

Checklist

✓ A percentage is just a fraction out of 100.

✓ A decimal fraction is just a decimal number with decimal places after the zero.

Worked examples

To convert fractions to percentages, multiply by 100.

For example: $\frac{1}{5}$ as a percentage is $\frac{1}{5} \times 100 = 20\%$

$\frac{3}{20}$ as a percentage is $\frac{3}{20} \times 100 = 15\%$

To convert a percentage to a fraction, write the percentage as a fraction with 100 as the denominator and simplify.

For example: 30% as a fraction is $\frac{30}{100} = \frac{3}{10}$

75% as a fraction is $\frac{75}{100} = \frac{3}{4}$

As percentages are in hundredths, they can easily be written as decimal fractions, using the tenths and hundredths column.

For example: 30% as a decimal is 0.30 (or 0.3)

75% as a decimal is 0.75

Now it's your turn!

47 A shop sale is offering 15% off all prices. How much will a £75 jacket cost in the sale? __£63.75__   (4)   *7.5 + 3.75 = 11.25*

48 A savings account pays interest at a rate of 1.5% each year. How much interest will Tom get after putting £5000 into this account for one year? __£75__

49 A large jar of coffee costs £5.50. If the price of coffee is increased by 2%, what will be the new price of a large jar? __£5.65__

50 A concert hall can sit 600 people. If 88% of the seats are sold, how many seats are still available? __72__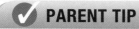

✓ PARENT TIP

Use SALE signs to work out a sale price when given a certain percentage off!

(K) Ratios

A ratio is the comparison of two or more numbers indicating their relative size. So, if two quantities are in the ratio 1 : 3, the second quantity is three times the size of the first. To divide a whole into two parts in the ratio 1 : 3, the whole has to be divided into four equal parts, with the first portion having one of those parts, and the second portion having three of those parts.

Worked example

If 4680 is shared in the ratio of 2 : 3 : 4, what is the value of each portion?

Total number of parts:	$2 + 3 + 4 = 9$
Whole amount divided into 9 parts:	$4680 \div 9 = 520$
The three portions will be:	$(2 \times 520) : (3 \times 520) : (4 \times 520)$
	1040 : 1560 : 2080

To express two quantities as a ratio, you must reduce the two numbers to their lowest terms. As with fractions, you do this by finding common factors and dividing both numbers by the same factor, until there are no further common factors. The ratio is then in its lowest terms. This may be referred to as simplifying or reducing a ratio. The same method is used for three or more quantities.

Worked examples

1 What is the ratio of 350 to 625?

Both are divisible by 5:	$350 \rightarrow 70$	:	$625 \rightarrow 125$
Both are divisible by 5 again:	$70 \rightarrow 14$	:	$125 \rightarrow 25$

14 and 25 have no other common factors (excluding 1) so the ratio is in its lowest form, and the answer will be written as **14 : 25**

2 Tom is 4 years older than Ben and 2 years younger that Sam, who is 11. They share 1000 marbles in the ratio of their ages. How many marbles do they each get?

Work out their ages to get the ratio:

Sam is 11 : Tom is 9 : Ben is 5

So, 1000 is to be shared in the ratio 11 : 9 : 5

Total of 25 parts, with each part being $\frac{1000}{25} = 40$

Sam will receive $(40 \times 11) = $ **440 marbles**

Tom will receive $(40 \times 9) = $ **360 marbles**

Ben will receive $(40 \times 5) = $ **200 marbles**   *Check your calculations by adding up the totals to make sure you get 1000!*

When maps or plans are drawn to scale, ratios are used to work out the length of lines on the plan.

If a map has a scale of 1 : 1000, for every 1000 m on the ground a line of 1 m would be drawn on the plan.

With a scale of 1 : 100,000, 1 km on the ground will be 1 cm on the map, as 1 km = 1000 m = 100,000 cm.

Worked example

How many km are represented by a line 2.5 cm long on a map with a scale of 1 : 50,000?

1 cm on the map represents 50,000 cm on the ground.

50,000 cm	=	500 m
500 m	=	0.5 km

So:	1 cm	represents	0.5 km
	2 cm	represents	1.0 km
	0.5 cm	represents	0.25 km
	2.5 cm	**represents**	**1.25 km**

Now it's your turn!

51 Share £4600 in the ratio 5 : 3 : 2 £420 : £1,533.33 : £2,300 (1)

52 An amount of money is shared between four children according to their ages, (2) which are 12, 10, 8, and 5 years respectively. The youngest child received £1000.

    a How much did the other three children each receive? 10 = £2000 / 8 = £1600

    12 = £2400

    b What was the total amount of money? £6000

53 A recipe uses a ratio of 3 : 2 : 1 of flour : butter : sugar. (1)

    If Lara has 200 g of butter, how much flour and sugar will she need?

    100 g of sugar and 300 g of flour

54 What distance is represented by 3 cm on a map with a scale of 1 : 250,000? (1)

    750,000 cm

L Decimals (including money)

Decimals are the numbers used in our base 10 number system, though the name decimal number is often used just to refer to a number that has a decimal point.

When solving problems with decimal numbers, remember to keep the decimal point in line when setting out the calculation!

Worked example

What is the total amount of fuel sold after four customers have purchased 34.14 litres, 56 litres, 32.68 litres and 15.7 litres of fuel respectively?

```
  3 4 . 1 4
  5 6 . 0 0 ←──────┐  Add the zeros in here to keep the decimal points aligned
  3 2 . 6 8        │
  1 5 . 7 0 ←──────┘
1 3 8 . 5 2 litres
  1   1   1
```

The metric system of measurement uses decimals (see section 3A Units for more detail), and most systems of money use a decimal system:

£1 = 100p   with £ often written as £1.00 with two decimal places, the tenths and hundredths for the pence that make up a pound.

REMEMBER!

When solving problems with money, remember to write all the prices in the same format!

Worked example

What change does Sam get from a £20 note after spending 92p on bread and £1.25 on a paper?

Express 92p as a decimal → £0.92, so 92p and £1.25 is   £0.92 + £1.25 = £2.17

£20 less £2.17 is   £20.00 – £2.17 = **£17.83**

Problems involving money often have amounts ending in 99p, for example £12.99 or £24.99.

When doing calculations involving costs ending in 99p, round up to the next pound to do the calculation, then subtract the number of pence from the answer.

Now it's your turn!

55 Faruq buys a shirt for £24.99 and a pair of shoes for £19.99. What is the total cost of his shopping? *£44.98*   (4)

56 Twenty-four children in a class each bring in 35p for a charity. How much do they collect? *£8.40*

57 A household uses 46.5 litres of water every day. If 10 litres costs 60p, how much does their water cost every day? *£2.79*

58 Sally has to have a 5 ml dose of medicine three times a day for 10 days. If a 300 ml bottle of the medicine costs £4.20, how much does the medicine cost per day? *21 p*

```
    ¹²
    2 4
  x  3 5
  ───────
  1 2 0
    7 29
  8.4 0

  £2.4 0
  £2.7 0
  £2.7 6
  £2.7 9
```

How Did You Do?

In this section there were 74 marks available in the 'Now it's your turn!' exercises. Check your answers against the list on page 94. How many did you score?

- 65 or fewer correct? Work through the question types again and make sure that you fully understand each section. Once you have done this, try the questions again before you move on.
- 66 correct or more. Well done! Do check any questions that were incorrect and make sure you understand where you made mistakes and why. Here is a number test with a mixture of questions for you to try.

Number test

1 What is the total of CCXI + LIV in Roman numerals? _____   ◯ 1

2 What are the next two numbers in this sequence?

   1   3   6   10   15   _____   _____   ◯ 1

3 1903 − 626 = _____

4 284 + 62 + 371 = _____

5 (48 ÷ 8) + (35 − 7) − (4 × 7) = _____

6 $\frac{10854}{2}$ − 407 = _____   ◯ 4

7 Underline the numbers which are multiples of 9.

   41   81   96   118   135   207   345

8 Which of these numbers are multiples of 3 and 7? Underline the answers.

   24   30   49   63   72   ◯ 2

9 Give two pairs of factors for each of these numbers.

   a 42 _____

   b 35 _____

   c 24 _____   ◯ 3

10 Write the square root of these numbers

   a 121 _____   **b** 36 _____   **c** 10,000 _____   ◯ 3

11 Order these numbers from smallest to biggest.

   0.1053   0.127   0.1309   0.129   0.109

   _____   ◯ 1

12 Round these numbers to the nearest hundred.

   a 2954 _____

   b 10,082 _____

   c 64 _____

   d 8888 _____

   e 2,999,967 _____ ◯ 5

13 Select from the following fractions and mixed numbers to complete the questions below. Any fraction or mixed number can only be used once and not all are used.

$\frac{4}{5}$	$5\frac{1}{9}$	$\frac{28}{32}$	$4\frac{1}{4}$	$\frac{10}{4}$	$5\frac{2}{9}$
$\frac{1}{18}$	$30\frac{1}{2}$	$\frac{2}{18}$	$\frac{6}{15}$	$\frac{9}{10}$	$31\frac{1}{2}$

   a Simplify $\frac{16}{20}$ = _____   **e** Equivalent to $\frac{7}{8}$ = _____

   b $\frac{7}{2} + \frac{3}{4}$ = _____   **f** $\frac{3}{5} + \frac{3}{10}$ = _____

   c $3\frac{2}{3} + 1\frac{4}{9}$ = _____   **g** $\frac{47}{9}$ as a mixed number = _____

   d $\frac{14}{20} \times 45$ = _____   **h** $\frac{1}{2} \times \frac{4}{36}$ = _____ ◯ 8

14 What is 15% of £125? _____

15 What is $\frac{56}{70}$ as a %? _____

16 If 60% of a bill is £204, what is the total bill? _____ ◯ 3

17 Express these ratios in their lowest terms.

   a 18 : 12 : 33 _____

   b 112 : 64 : 40 _____

   c 13 : 65 : 39 _____ ◯ 3

18 What distance on a map of scale 1 : 50,000 represents

   1 km? _____

19 How far on the ground is 15 cm on a map of scale

   1 : 20,000? _____ ◯ 2

20 240.4 − 153.25 = _____

21 0.79 + 3.7 + 7. 39 = _____ ◯ 2

22 How much change will I get from a £20 note after spending £2.99

   and £1.85? _____

23 Share £11,205 equally between 6. _____

24 What is the value of the largest share when £80,100 is shared in

   the ratio 1 : 3 : 5? _____ ◯ 3

Ⓐ Angles

Angles occur when two straight lines meet at a point. Angles also measure the amount of turn.

Angles are measured in degrees, with one complete turn, or circle, being divided into 360 degrees (360°).

Checklist

- ✓ An **acute angle** is an angle measuring less than 90°
- ✓ A **right angle** is a 'square' corner and measures exactly 90°
- ✓ An **obtuse angle** is greater than 90° and less than 180°
- ✓ An angle of exactly 180° forms a straight line
- ✓ A **reflex angle** is greater than 180° and less than 360°

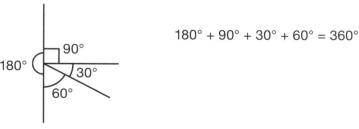

| Acute angle < 90° | Right angle 90° | Obtuse angle > 90° < 180° | Straight line 180° | Reflex angle > 180° < 360° |

There are some simple rules to learn to be able to calculate angles in given shapes and patterns.

1 The three angles of a triangle always add up to 180°

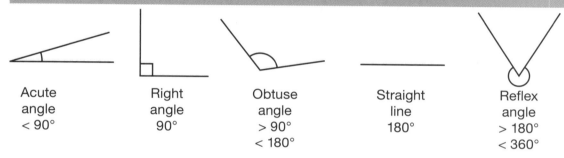

93° + 52° + 35° = 180°

2 The angles on a straight line add up to 180°

5° + 65° + 110° = 180°

3 Angles around a point add up to 360°

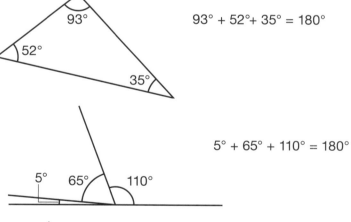

180° + 90° + 30° + 60° = 360°

4 The four angles in a quadrilateral add up to 360°

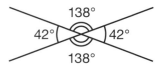

90° + 90° + 90° + 90° = 360°

110° + 105° + 70° + 75° = 360°

5 Vertically opposite angles are equal.

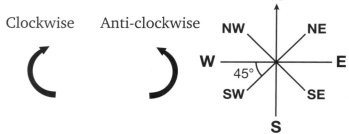

When measuring 'turns', the points of the compass are often used to indicate direction faced, and the terms 'clockwise' and 'anti-clockwise' are used to indicate the direction of turn.

REMEMBER!

Remember that there are 45° between each of the eight points of the compass.

Clockwise   Anti-clockwise

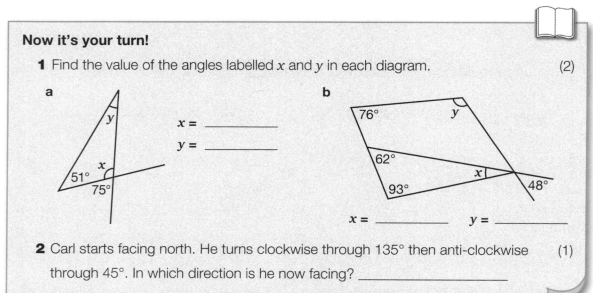

Now it's your turn!

1 Find the value of the angles labelled x and y in each diagram. (2)

a

x = _____

y = _____

b

x = _____   y = _____

2 Carl starts facing north. He turns clockwise through 135° then anti-clockwise (1) through 45°. In which direction is he now facing? _____

B Two-dimensional shapes (polygons)

A 2-D shape, or polygon, can be described by its angles and sides.

Triangles have 3 angles and 3 sides and their internal angles add up to 180°.

Types of triangles:

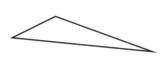

| Equilateral | Isoceles | Right-angled | Scalene |

Notice the different properties of the triangles, especially where the sides are equal in length and where there are equal angles.

Quadrilaterals all have 4 angles and 4 sides and their internal angles add up to 360°.

Types of quadrilaterals:

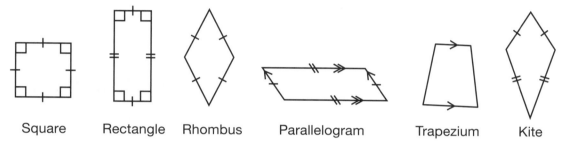

| Square | Rectangle | Rhombus | Parallelogram | Trapezium | Kite |

Other common 2-D shapes	Less common 2-D shapes
A pentagon has 5 angles and 5 sides.	A heptagon has 7 angles and 7 sides.
A hexagon has 6 angles and 6 sides.	A nonagon has 9 angles and 9 sides.
An octagon has 8 angles and 8 sides.	A decagon has 10 angles and 10 sides.

Circles are 2-D shapes with one curved line, no straight edges and no corners.
A straight line from the centre of the circle to its edge is called the radius, and the straight line distance across the circle, passing through the centre, is called its diameter.

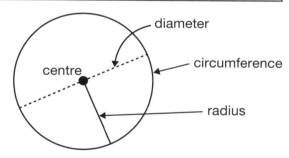

C Three-dimensional shapes (polyhedra) and nets

There are a number of three-dimensional (3-D) shapes, or solids (also called polyhedra), that you need to be able to recognise. They can be described by their properties – number and type of faces, edges and corners (or vertices).

sphere	1 curved surface
cone	a flat circular base, 1 curved surface, 1 curved edge and 1 vertex
cylinder	2 flat circular faces and 1 curved surface, 2 curved edges and no vertices
cuboid	6 rectangular faces with opposite faces identical, 12 edges and 8 vertices
cube	6 identical square faces (a, 12 edges and 8 vertices (*a cube is a special cuboid*)

Sphere   Cone   Cylinder   Cube

Cuboid

prism	2 identical polygons at each end, with faces joined by parallelograms between corresponding vertices. A prism is described by the shape of the polygon, for example, a hexagonal prism. (*A cylinder and a cuboid are special prisms.*)
pyramid	A flat base with triangular side faces meeting at a point. This point is perpendicular to the centre of the base shape in a 'right' pyramid. The shape of the base surface describes the pyramid, for example, a triangular-based pyramid, a square-based pyramid.

Eg.

Pentagonal prism   Triangular-based pyramid   Square-based pyramid

REMEMBER!

The net of a solid is a 2-D plan which, if cut out and folded, would construct a given 3-D shape. Some non-verbal reasoning questions require you to identify which cubes could, or could not, be made from a given net. (See F6 Nets in the non-verbal reasoning skills section for more help on this question type.)

✔ PARENT TIP

How many different 3-D shapes can be identified going round the supermarket?

Now it's your turn!

3 What is the value of the angle marked x in each of these diagrams?   (3)

a

76°

115° x

x = _____

b

x

135°

85°   88°

x = _____

c

x

70°   148°

x = _____

4 What is the total surface area of this solid?   (1)

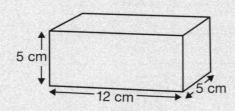

5 cm

12 cm   5 cm

Surface area = _____

5 What is the name of a solid shape with four triangular faces and one square surface? _____ (1)

6 Which of these nets could be folded up to give a cube? Underline the correct answer. (1)

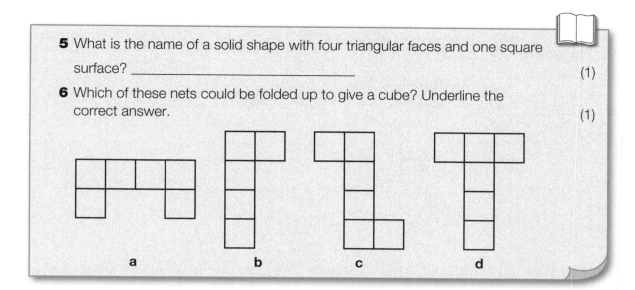

a   b   c   d

D Perimeter

The perimeter of any shape is the total distance around the edge (for a circle this is called its circumference).

You need to apply your knowledge of 2-D shapes to work out the lengths of different sides. For example, all four sides of a square are the same length, and a rectangle has two pairs of sides of equal length.

> **REMEMBER!**
>
> When calculating the perimeter around a shape made up of more than one side, you need to check that each length is given in the same units.

Worked examples

1 What is the perimeter of a rectangle that is twice as long as it is wide, and has a width of 16 cm?

width = 16 cm   length = (16×2) cm = 32 cm

$$\text{perimeter} = (2 \times \text{width}) + (2 \times \text{length})$$
$$= 32 \text{ cm} + 64 \text{ cm}$$
$$= \textbf{96 cm}$$

2 What is the perimeter of a regular octagon with 3.5 cm sides?

octagon has eight sides, so perimeter
$$= 8 \times 3.5 \text{ cm}$$
$$= \textbf{28 cm}$$

For an irregular shape made up of rectangles, you may have to calculate some lengths before being able to work out the perimeter.

Worked example

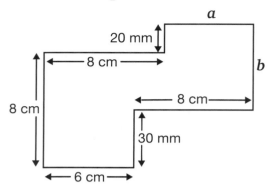

From this diagram the unknown lengths can be calculated: $a = (6 + 8) - 8 = 6\,cm$
(Remember to convert all lengths into the same unit.) $b = (8 + 2) - 3 = 7\,cm$
So the perimeter of this shape is $(8 + 8 + 2 + 6 + 8 + 3 + 7 + 6)\,cm = \mathbf{48\,cm}$

(E) Area

Area is a measure of a surface. It is measured in square units.

The area of a rectangle is found by multiplying the length by the width.

> **REMEMBER!**
>
> Remember to convert all lengths used in an area calculation into the same units!

Both measurements need to be in the same units, so if the measurements are in centimetres (cm), the area calculated will be in square centimetres (cm^2).

To find the area of a triangle, you need to know the measurement of its perpendicular height. In a right-angled triangle, this will be the side that forms a right angle with the base.

> **REMEMBER!**
>
> If asked to find the area of an irregular shape it is often helpful to sketch a diagram and note the different measurements.

area of a triangle $= \frac{1}{2} \times$ base $\times$ height

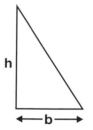 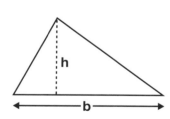 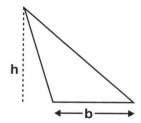

Area $= \frac{1}{2} \times b \times h$

Now it's your turn!

7 What shape has sides of equal length, each 3.5 cm long, and a perimeter of   (1)
     24.5 cm? _____

8 What is the perimeter of a 14 cm-wide rectangle that is twice as long as it   (1)
     is wide? _____

9 What is the total surface area of a 4 cm cube? _____   (1)

---

10 How much wire is needed to make a two-strand fence around this field, excluding the gates? _____ (1)

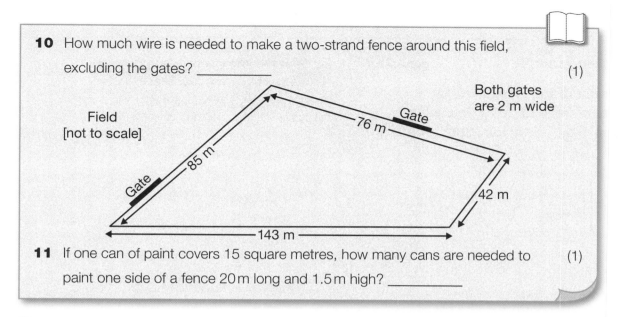

Field
[not to scale]

Both gates
are 2 m wide

Gate

76 m

85 m

Gate

42 m

143 m

11 If one can of paint covers 15 square metres, how many cans are needed to (1) paint one side of a fence 20 m long and 1.5 m high? _____

⒡ *Volume and capacity*

Volume and capacity are very closely related, but they use different units of measurement.

Volume is measured in cubic units and is the measurement of an amount of space or within a solid shape.

Capacity is also the measure of volume, but it is measured in litres as opposed to cubic units. It is used to measure the volume of a liquid, which is something that takes on the shape of the container into which it is poured.

Checklist

✓ Volume is a measure of the amount of space in a three-dimensional solid.
✓ Volume is measured in cubic units.
✓ For a regular cuboid, it is found by multiplying the length × width × height.
✓ Remember that all measurements used in the calculation must be in the same units.

Worked example

What is the volume of a cuboid 3 cm wide, 5 cm high and 10 cm long?

Volume = length × width × height
       = 10 cm × 3 cm × 5 cm = **150 cm³**

The metric units used to measure capacity are litres (l). Each litre can be subdivided into 1000 millilitres.

There is a complex formula for calculating the volume of a sphere, but you can work out how many balls or spheres can fit into a box if you know the diameter of the sphere, as you take the diameter to be the measure of the length, width and height of the sphere, that is, the cubic space into which the ball would sit.

Worked example

How many tennis balls with a diameter of 8 cm can fit into a box 16 cm deep, 35 cm long and 10 cm wide?

REMEMBER!

Drawing a sketch often helps to visualise what you need to calculate.

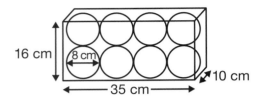

16 cm | 8 cm | 10 cm | 35 cm

How many balls can fit along the box's length?	35 cm ÷ 8 = 4 (with a remainder of 3 cm)
How many balls can fit across its width?	10 cm ÷ 8 = 1 (with a remainder of 2 cm)
How many layers can fit in its depth?	16 cm ÷ 8 = 2 (no remainder)

Total number of balls is: $4 \times 1 \times 2 = \textbf{8 balls}$

Now it's your turn!

12 How many millilitres are in the following amounts?   (3)

    a 2.4 litres _____   **b** $\frac{3}{4}$ of a litre _____   **c** 3.75 litres? _____

13 A crate with a volume of 7.5 cubic metres is 125 cm wide and 2 metres long.   (1)
    How high is it? _____

14 How many packs of cards 1 cm × 5 cm × 8 cm will fit into a box 40 cm long,   (1)
    20 cm wide and 3 cm deep? _____

(G) Symmetry

Line symmetry or reflection

This is the type of symmetry that you will come across most often in assessment papers.

A shape that has lines of symmetry has a line where it can be folded and where each part is a reflection of the other part. Shapes can have more than one line of symmetry, and the line of symmetry may pass through a shape or be beside it.

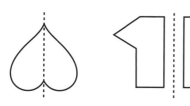 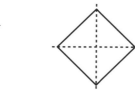 

 = lines of symmetry or

Rotational symmetry

A shape has rotational symmetry when the shape or pattern can be rotated through a number of degrees and then fit into exactly the same shape as when in the previous position.

 rotate through 120° clockwise

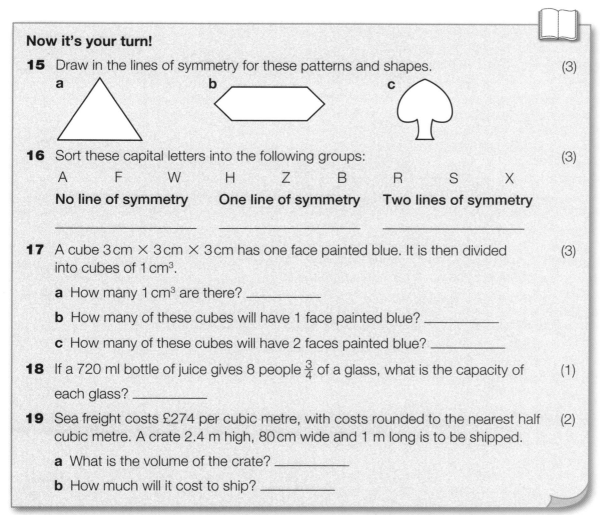

Now it's your turn!

15 Draw in the lines of symmetry for these patterns and shapes. (3)

   a   **b**   **c**

16 Sort these capital letters into the following groups: (3)

    A   F   W   H   Z   B   R   S   X

   No line of symmetry   **One line of symmetry**   **Two lines of symmetry**

   _____   _____   _____

17 A cube 3 cm × 3 cm × 3 cm has one face painted blue. It is then divided (3) into cubes of 1 cm³.

   a How many 1 cm³ are there? _____

   b How many of these cubes will have 1 face painted blue? _____

   c How many of these cubes will have 2 faces painted blue? _____

18 If a 720 ml bottle of juice gives 8 people $\frac{3}{4}$ of a glass, what is the capacity of (1) each glass? _____

19 Sea freight costs £274 per cubic metre, with costs rounded to the nearest half (2) cubic metre. A crate 2.4 m high, 80 cm wide and 1 m long is to be shipped.

   a What is the volume of the crate? _____

   b How much will it cost to ship? _____

20 Complete this grid so that it has 2 lines of symmetry: (1)

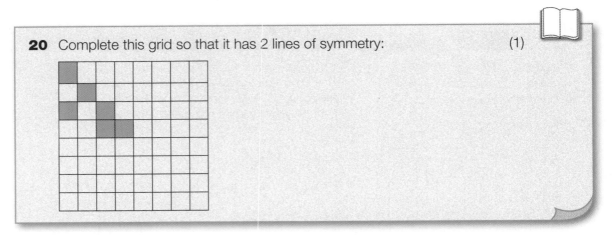

How did you do?

In this section there were 32 marks available in the 'Now it's your turn!' exercises. Check your answers against the list on page 95. How many did you score?

- 25 or fewer correct? Work through the question types again and make sure that you fully understand each section. Once you have done this, try the questions again before you move on.
- 26 correct or more. Well done! Do check any questions that were incorrect and make sure you understand where you made mistakes and why. Here is a shape and space test with a mixture of questions for you to try.

Shape and space test

1 Calculate the value of angle x in each of these diagrams.

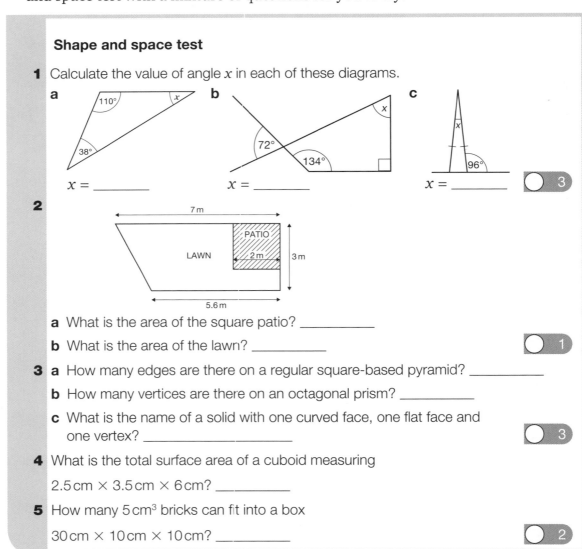

a $x =$ _____

b $x =$ _____

c $x =$ _____   3

2

a What is the area of the square patio? _____

b What is the area of the lawn? _____   1

3 a How many edges are there on a regular square-based pyramid? _____

b How many vertices are there on an octagonal prism? _____

c What is the name of a solid with one curved face, one flat face and one vertex? _____   3

4 What is the total surface area of a cuboid measuring

2.5 cm × 3.5 cm × 6 cm? _____

5 How many 5 cm³ bricks can fit into a box

30 cm × 10 cm × 10 cm? _____   2

6 Name each of these polygons and state how many lines of symmetry they each have.

a

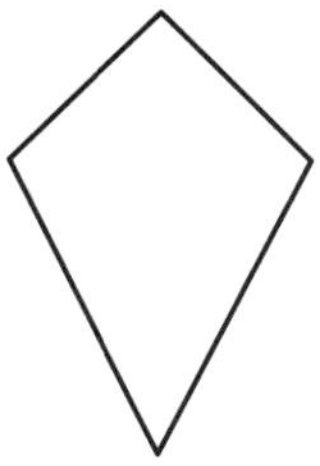

Name: _____

Lines of symmetry: _____

b

Name: _____

Lines of symmetry: _____

c

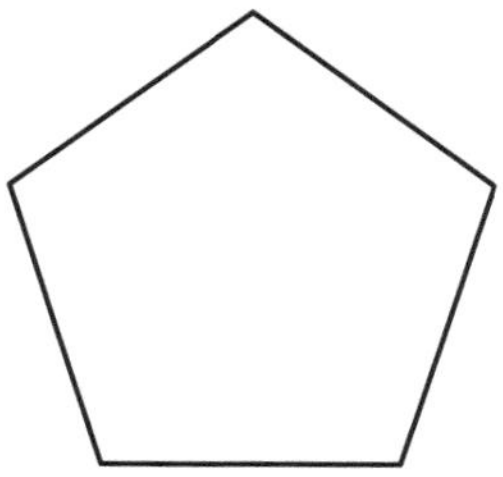

Name: _____

Lines of symmetry: _____

◯ 6

7 What is the volume of this tank? _____

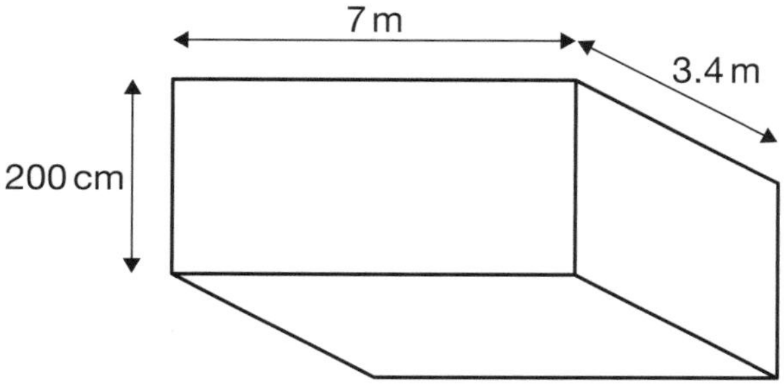

7 m

3.4 m

200 cm

◯ 1

8 What type of polyhedron (solid shape) is made when this net is folded along the dotted lines? _____

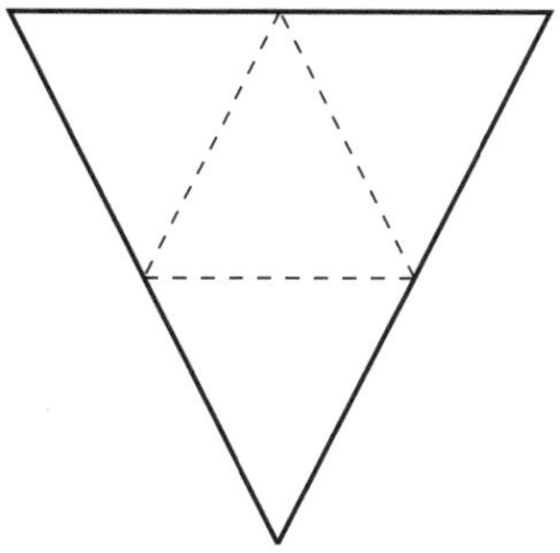

◯ 1

9 What is the area of the shaded sections in these diagrams?

a

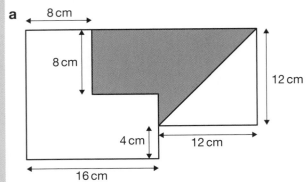

Area: _____

b

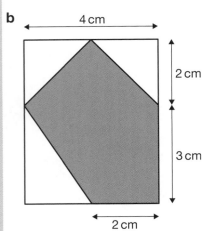

Area: _____

 4

10 a How many balls with a radius of 5 cm will fit into a 50 cm × 30 cm × 70 cm box?

_____

b If the balls were only 4 cm in diameter, how many would fit into the same box?

_____

2

11 What is the size of the obtuse angle in each of these diagrams?

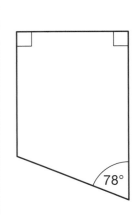

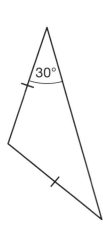

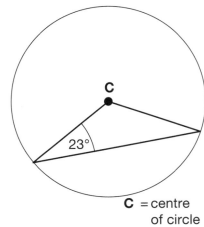

C = centre
of circle

a _____   **b** _____   **c** _____   3

3 Measure

(A) Units

Metric units use some common prefixes – learn these well!

milli is for $\frac{1}{1000}$	centi is for $\frac{1}{100}$	kilo is for $\times$ 1000

1000 millimetres	= 1 metre	= 100 centimetres	
	1000 metres		= 1 kilometre
1000 millilitres	= 1 litre		
1000 milligrams	= 1 gram		
	1000 grams		= 1 kilogram

When solving problems with mixed units, remember this checklist:

Checklist

- ✓ Convert them all to the same unit before doing any calculation.
- ✓ Keep the decimal point in line when setting out a block sum.
- ✓ Show the units in the answer.

Worked example

How many cm are there in 35.2 cm + 3.03 m + 55 mm?

Convert all to cm: 35.2 + 303 + 5.5

Add together: 343.7

Show units in answer: **343.7 cm**

```
    3   5   .   2
3   0   3   .   3
            5   .   5
  _____
3   4₁  3   .   7
```

Most of the questions you will come across in CEM and other assessment papers will use metric measurements, but occasionally the old imperial units are used. Here are the ones that you might need to know:

length	inch (ins or ″)	foot (ft or ′)	yard (yd)	mile (mi or m*)
	12 inches	= 1 foot		(* an m can also indicate metres, so read the question carefully to find other clues to work out which unit is being used)
	3 feet	= 1 yard		
	1760 yards	= 1 mile		
mass	ounce (oz)	pound (lb)	16 ounces	= 1 pound
capacity	pint (pt)	gallon (gal)	8 pints	= 1 gallon

See sections 3B, 3C and 3D below for information about the units for time, speed and temperature.

Now it's your turn!

1 Sharon cuts two pieces of ribbon, one 45 cm long and the other 1.60 m long. (3)
If there was 3 m on the reel of ribbon at the start, how much is left? _____

2 If 1 kg is approximately 2.2 lbs, and there are 16 ounces in a pound,
approximately how many ounces are there in 5 kg? _____

3 If there are four 750 ml bottles of juice, how many 150 ml glasses can be
filled? _____

(B) Time

The measurement of time is not based on a decimal system.

60 seconds	=	1 minute
60 minutes	=	1 hour
24 hours	=	1 day
7 days	=	1 week
365 days	=	1 year (*except a leap year which has 366 days*)

Worked example

Add together 2 hours 32 minutes and 40 seconds and 3 hour 45 minutes and 30 seconds.

Add the seconds together	40 + 30 = 70
Divide by 60 to convert to minutes	70 ÷ 60 = 1 remainder 10*, that is 1 minute and 10 seconds
Add together the minutes	32 + 45 = 77
Divide by 60 to convert to hours	77 ÷ 60 = 1 remainder 17*, that is 1 hour and 17 minutes
	Remember you cannot add a decimal point and carry on dividing
Add together the hours	2 + 3 = 5 that is 5 hours

Add the three parts together to get the final total: 5 hours + 1 hour 17 minutes + 1 minute 10 seconds = **6 hours 18 minutes 10 seconds**

Times of day can be given using the 12-hour clock or the 24-hour clock.

With the 12-hour clock, the suffix 'am' or 'pm' must be used. A clock that tells the time with a traditional clock face is called an analogue clock. Clocks that tell the time using the 24-hour clock are called digital clocks.

Reading times from an analogue clock may refer to the number of minutes to the hour when the time is after half past. Times may also use 'quarter to', 'quarter past' and 'half past'. Remembering that there are 60 minutes in an hour, 'quarter to' is 15 minutes before the hour, 'quarter past' is 15 minutes past and 'half past' is 30 minutes past.

If the time is given as half past two, look carefully at the question to find an indication of whether this is in the morning, 2:30am, or afternoon, 2:30pm.

 **PARENT TIP**

Practise calculating the duration of different TV programmes from a TV guide.

REMEMBER!

12:00 is midday and 00:00 is midnight. Times written in the 24-hour clock do not use am and pm, and are always written with four digits.

Now it's your turn!

4–8 Change one format to another to complete this table. (5)

Time in words	12-hour clock	24-hour clock
Half past three in the afternoon		
Twenty to eleven in the evening		
Quarter to nine in the morning		
		19:05
	11:59am	

REMEMBER!

Remember that 0.5h is 30 minutes!

Now it's your turn!

Solve these problems, which are all about time. (3)

9 Convert 4500 seconds to hours, minutes and seconds. _____

10 A train leaves the station at 17:16 and takes 47 minutes to get to Alston. At what time will it arrive at Alston? _____

11 If the tide takes 6 hours and 11 minutes to come in, and it is low tide at 6:20am, at what time will it next be high tide? _____

C *Speed*

REMEMBER!

Miles per hour is one of the most commonly used of the old imperial units.

Speed is the measure of distance travelled in a given time.

The most common units used to measure speed are km per hour (km/h or km/hour) or miles per hour (mph or miles/hour).

When solving problems involving speed, think carefully about the units that are being used.

Worked example

If a car is travelling at 30 mph, how far does it travel in 30 minutes?

30 minutes is half an hour, so the car will travel 15 miles in half an hour.

If the question asks how far will the car travel in 20 minutes, remember 20 minutes is one-third of an hour, so the car travelling at 30 mph will cover $\frac{1}{3} \times 30$ miles, which is **10 miles** in the 20 minutes.

If a question tells you how long a journey takes and the distance covered, the distance divided by the time take will give an average speed for the journey. Remember again to check the units so that your answer is in the form asked for.

Worked example

What is a lorry's average speed if it takes $4\frac{1}{2}$ hours to cover 288 miles?

Average speed in mph $= \dfrac{\text{distance in miles}}{\text{time in hours}}$

$= \frac{288}{4.5}$ mph multiply top and bottom by 2 to make the bottom number a whole number

$= \frac{576}{9}$ mph

$=$ **64 mph**

Measuring the speed of smaller objects over shorter distances may use units such as metres per second.

Apply the same processes, remembering that speed = distance divided by time, checking the units carefully.

Now it's your turn!

12 What is the average speed of a car on a journey of 58 miles if the journey takes (4)
1 hour 20 minutes? _____

13 How long will it take to reach a destination 84 km away if the train has an average speed of 126 km/h? _____

14 A toy car covers a 30 m track in 6 seconds. What is its average speed in metres per second? _____

15 What distance does an aircraft cover in $3\frac{1}{2}$ hours if its average speed is 480 mph? _____

(D) Temperature

Temperature is measured in degrees. Degrees Celsius (°C) are the units most commonly used, though you may come across use of degrees Fahrenheit (°F).

With the Celsius scale (sometimes also called centigrade), 0°C is the freezing point of water and 100°C is the boiling point of water.

When the temperature falls below freezing point, negative numbers are used to indicate the temperature.

Worked examples

A temperature of −10°C is 10 degrees below freezing.

If the temperature then increases by 12 degrees, it would rise to 2°C.

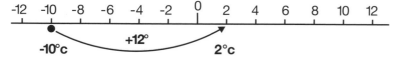

If the temperature is 6°C and it falls 13 degrees, the new temperature will be −7°C. A fall of 6°C takes the the temperature down to 0°C or freezing point, and then the fall of a further 7°C takes the temperature down to −7°C.

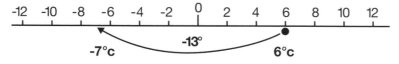

REMEMBER!

A graph can show negative numbers by extending the x-axis to the left of the zero and the y-axis below the zero.

Now it's your turn!

16–23 This table shows the changes in temperature in one day. Complete the missing numbers.   (8)

6:00am	9:00am	12:00 noon	3:00pm	6:00pm	9:00pm	midnight	3:00am	6:00am
3°C								
Change	+2°C	+4°C	+1°C	−4°C	−4°C	−3°C	−2°C	+1°C

How did you do?

In this section there were 23 marks available in the 'Now it's your turn!' exercises. Check your answers against the list on page 95. How many did you score?

- 17 or fewer correct? Work through the question types again and make sure that you fully understand each section. Once you have done this, try the questions again before you move on.
- 18 correct or more. Well done! Do check any questions that were incorrect and make sure you understand where you made mistakes and why. Here is a measure test with a mixture of questions for you to try.

Measure test

1 If a journey on the train takes 1 hour 27 minutes, when will each of these trains arrive at the destination?

Depart: **a** 10:48   Arrive: _____

b 13:03   Arrive: _____

c 16:38   Arrive: _____

d 20:51   Arrive: _____   ◯ 4

2 Complete these equations.

a 720 ml = _____ litres

b 53 mm = _____ cm = **c** _____ metres

d 10 kg = _____ g

e 1.3 km = _____ cm

f 17.03 m = _____ mm = **g** _____ km = **h** _____ cm   ◯ 5

3 If 1 pint is approximately 0.57 litres, how many ml are there in a

gallon? _____   ◯ 1

4 How long are the following programmes?

a Start: 05:25   End: 06:12   _____ minutes

b Start: 22:54   End: 23:32   _____ minutes

c Start: 15:05   End: 16:28   _____ minutes   ◯ 3

5 Answer the following questions about this timetable, which shows the different lessons each morning of the week.

	Monday	Tuesday	Wednesday	Thursday	Friday
9:00	English	Maths	Maths	English	Maths
9:45	History	English	RE	Geography	English
10:30	B	R	E	A	K
10:50	Maths	Science	English	Maths	Science
?	PE	Science	Spanish	Art	Music

a If all lessons are 45 minutes long, when does the art lesson start on a Thursday?

_____

b How long is the morning break? _____

c How much time is allocated to science each week? _____

Practice Test

CEM Maths and Non-verbal Reasoning

Read the instructions carefully.

This paper is designed to be completed in **45 minutes**, but the aim is to gain as many correct questions in the time. It may not be possible for you to complete every question in the time given, but working through the books that accompany this range will give you the opportunity to work to time and to gain the experience of each question type.

OXFORD
UNIVERSITY PRESS

Great Clarendon Street, Oxford, OX2 6DP, United Kingdom

Oxford University Press is a department of the University of Oxford.
It furthers the University's objective of excellence in research, scholarship, and education by publishing worldwide. Oxford is a registered trade mark of Oxford University Press in the UK and in certain other countries

Text © Alison Primrose 2015

Illustrations © Oxford University Press 2015

The moral rights of the author have been asserted

First published in 2015

British Library Cataloguing in Publication Data

Data available

978-0-1927-4289-6
10 9 8

Paper used in the production of this book is a natural, recyclable product made from wood grown in sustainable forests. The manufacturing process conforms to the environmental regulations of the country of origin.

Printed in China

Acknowledgements

Page make-up by Oxford Designers & Illustrators

1 Order these numbers from lowest value to highest:

46.92   46.69   64.69   49.01   62.14

_____

2 Which of the following numbers are multiples of 3 and 7? Underline the correct answers.

42   18   21   64   28   35   73

3 Complete the missing numbers.

a 583 + _____ = 800   **b** 174 x 3 = _____   **c** _____ ÷ 5 = 610

4 What is the perimeter of this shape? All measurements are in cm.

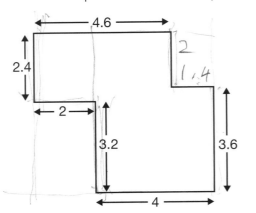

$\underline{26.2}$ cm

$3.2 + 2.4 = 3.6 + x$
$\boxed{3.6} + x = 5.6$ ✓
$x = 5.6 - 3.6$
$x = 2$
$4 + 2 = y + 4.6$
$y + \boxed{4.6} = 6$ ✓
$y = 6 - 4.6$
$y = 1.4$
$4 + 3.6 + 1.4 + 2 + 4.6 + 2.4 + 2$
$+ 3.2 = \underline{26.2 \, cm}$

5 How many cm altogether in 1.34 m, 50 mm and 42 cm? _____

6 If $y = 13$ and $z = \frac{1}{2}$, complete the following equations:

a $3y + 8z = \underline{43}$ **b** $4yz - \underline{6} = 20$ **c** $\frac{100}{z} + 2y = 100 + \underline{126}$

$3 \overset{\downarrow}{9} + \overset{\downarrow}{4} = 43$ $26 - 6 = 20$ $2\cancel{0}0 + \cancel{2}6 = 100 + \underline{126}$

7 90 cubes fit into a box 10 cm long and 12 cm wide. If each cube is $2 \times 2 \times 2$ cm,

how high is the box? _____

8 Circle the correct answer to this sum.

VIII + XX − XIX

8   21   49   9   48   19

9 Which number comes next in these sequences?

a 73, 69, 64, 58, 51, _____

b 103, 214, 325, 436, _____

c 2, 5, 10, 17, 26, 37, 50, _____

10 A bus sets out on a circular route at 11:24 and completes the circuit by 17:35.

How long does it take? _____

11 Complete this grid using the numbers 1, 3, 7, 8, 9, 10 and 11 so that all the rows and columns add up to 22.

5		
	12	

12 Write the names of these shapes.

a 3 sides, 2 of which are the same length _____

b 5 equal angles and 5 equal sides _____

13 Reduce these fractions to their simplest form.

a $\frac{42}{60}$ _____ **b** $\frac{24}{30}$ _____ **c** $\frac{33}{121}$ _____ **d** $\frac{16}{40}$ _____

14 What is 12% of £2,500? _____

15 Plot these points on the axes below and then join them up to form a shape.

A (2, 6)   B (4, 1)   C (4, 8)   D (6, 6)

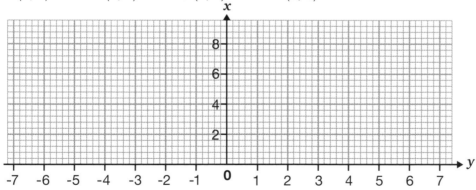

Reflect the shape in the *y*-axis.

What are the coordinates of the reflected shape?

A' _____   B' _____   C' _____   D' _____

8
TOTAL

16 A road consists of 4 layers. The base foundation is 1.1 m of gravel and sand, then there is a 14 cm layer of concrete, then a 2.6 cm layer of tarmac and lastly a 16 mm layer of waterproof paint.

What is the total depth of the road in cm? _____

2

17 There are flowerbeds 2 m wide all around a house, with a 2 m gap at the front door and a 1 m gap at the back door. The base of the house forms a rectangle 11 m by 8 m.

   a What length of the house wall is next to a flowerbed? _____

   b What is the total area of the flowerbeds? _____

3

18 There are 120 marbles in a jar. Half are red, 10% are blue, 38 are white and the rest are yellow.

   a How many yellow marbles are there in the jar? _____

12 more yellow marbles are added to the jar.

   b What fraction of the marbles in the jar will now be yellow? _____

   c If the red marbles are shared in the ratio of 1 : 2 : 3 between Ann, Tom and Ben,

      how many red marbles will Ben get? _____

3

19 A train travels at an average speed of 55 km/hour for the first 2 hours, then it stops for 20 minutes before continuing the journey at an average speed of 70 km/hour.

The total journey, including the stop, takes 3 hours 20 minutes.

   a How far does the train travel altogether? _____

   b How far does the train travel before it stops? _____

   c What fraction of the total journey time does the train spent stopped? _____

3

20 Toli's suitcase weighs 600 g when empty.

He packs a camera weighing 1.3 kg, a book weighing 220 g and 2 pairs of trousers weighing 380 g each. The weight limit for luggage is 20 kg.

   a What is the total weight of the contents in the suitcase in grams? _____

   b How much more can be added to the suitcase before it reaches the weight limit? Give your answer in kg.

      _____

3

Which one completes the second pair in the same way as the first pair?

21

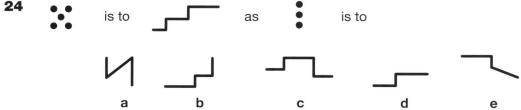

a   b   c   d   e

22

a   b   c   d   e

23

a   b   c   d   e

24

a   b   c   d   e

4

How To Do CEM Maths and Non-verbal Reasoning
© Oxford University Press, 2015

4
TOTAL

Which one belongs with the pair of shapes on the left?

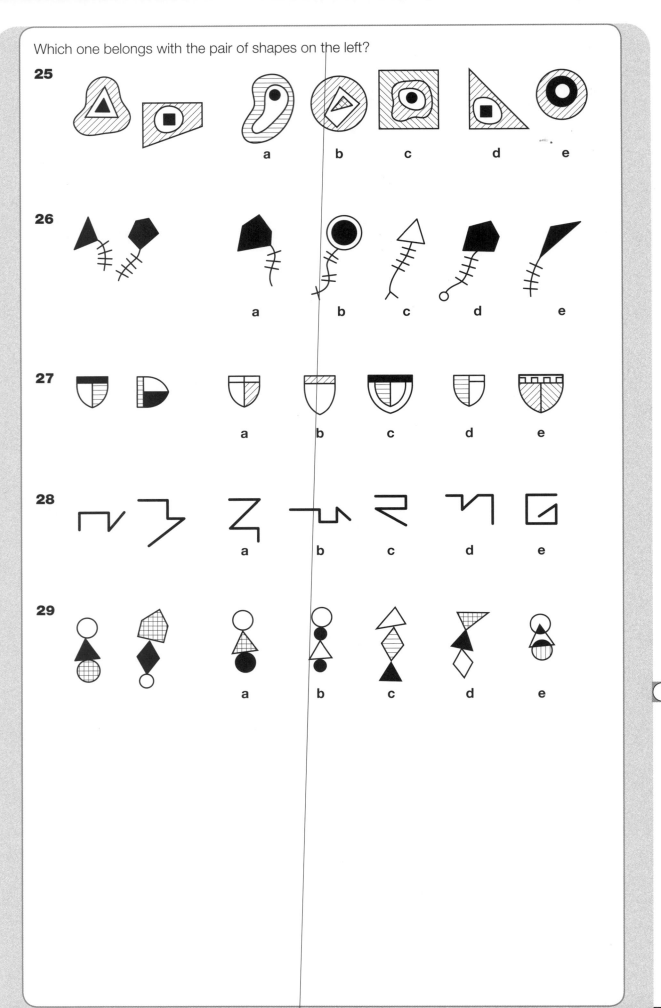

25

a   b   c   d   e

26

a   b   c   d   e

27

a   b   c   d   e

28

a   b   c   d   e

29

a   b   c   d   e

5

Which one comes next?

30

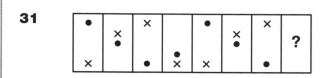

a   b   c   d   e

31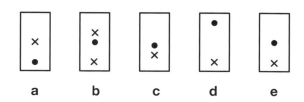

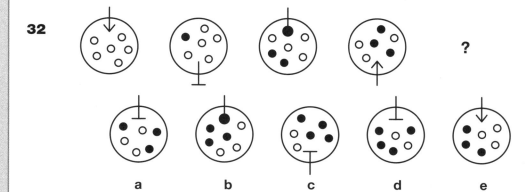

a   b   c   d   e

32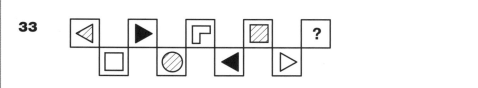

a   b   c   d   e

33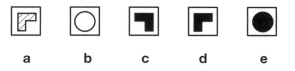

a   b   c   d   e

4

Which cube can be made from the given net?

34

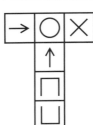

a b c d e

35

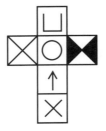

a b c d e

36

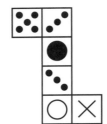

a b c d e

37

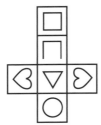

a b c d e

4

4
TOTAL

Which code matches the shape or pattern at the end of each line?

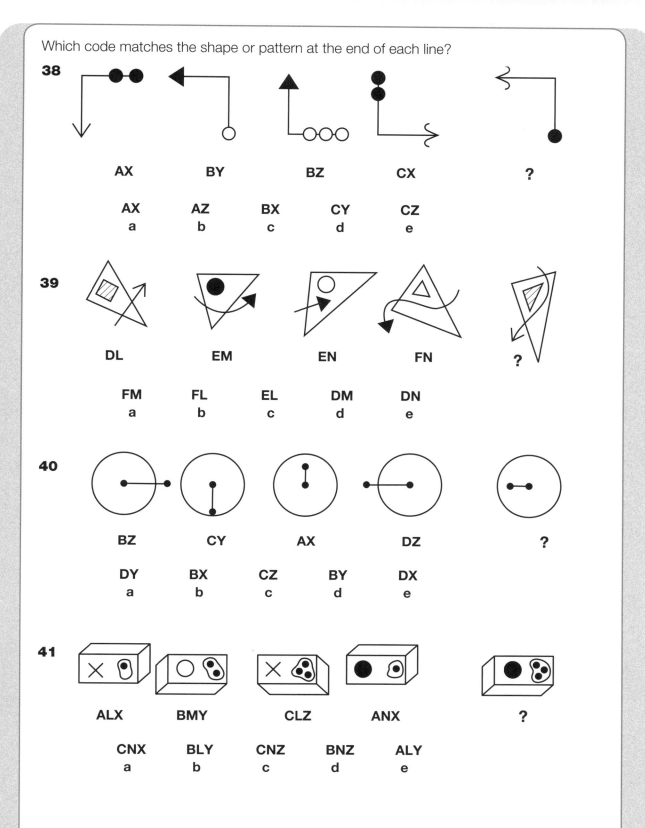

38

AX   BY   BZ   CX   ?

AX	AZ	BX	CY	CZ
a	b	c	d	e

39

DL   EM   EN   FN   ?

FM	FL	EL	DM	DN
a	b	c	d	e

40

BZ   CY   AX   DZ   ?

DY	BX	CZ	BY	DX
a	b	c	d	e

41

ALX   BMY   CLZ   ANX   ?

CNX	BLY	CNZ	BNZ	ALY
a	b	c	d	e

4
TOTAL

42 This pie chart shows the flavours of ice cream sold one day.

Ice Cream Flavour

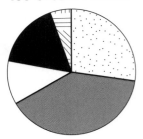

☐ Chocolate   ■ Vanilla   ☐ Strawberry
■ Mint Choc Chip   ◩ Mango

a Which flavour was the least popular? _____

b What flavour was the second most popular? _____

c Which two flavours combined form exactly half of the sales? _____

d If 10% of sales were strawberry, and 20 strawberry ice creams were sold,

   how many vanilla ice creams were sold? _____

4

43 This table shows the attendance register for one week for three classes in a school, where there are 30 children in each class.

	Monday	Tuesday	Wednesday	Thursday	Friday
Class A	28	29	25	29	29
Class B	30	30	28	29	28
Class C	26	27	29	28	30

a What was the average attendance for Class A that week? _____

b What is the mode of these attendance figures, looking at all three classes?

   _____

c Which day had the best attendance? _____

3

7
TOTAL

44   This graph shows the number of groups of children using the library.

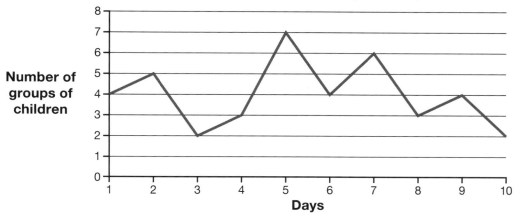

Number of groups of children

Days

a Which day(s) had the most groups? _____

b What was the average or mean number of groups using the library during those

10 days? _____

c On which days did 3 groups use the library? _____

d What was the maximum number of groups using the library in any one day?

_____

e How many groups used the library on day 4? _____

◯ 4

45   This table shows the marks for four students.

	Sam	Tilly	William	Yolanda
Paper 1	75%	66%	80%	78%
Paper 2	83%	92%	76%	85%

a From these test results, what was the range of marks on Paper 1?

_____

b What was the mean score for Paper 2? _____

c Who had the highest total score? _____

◯ 3

7
TOTAL

70
TOTAL

d What percentage of lessons on the morning timetable is given to English? _____

e If 10 minutes of each maths lesson is given to mental maths, how much time is spent on mental maths each week? _____ ⬤ 5

6 How far will each of these cars travel in $2\frac{1}{2}$ hours if their average speed is:

a 38 mph _____

b 54 km/h _____

c 70 mph _____ ⬤ 3

7 Work out the final temperature after these series of changes.

a 4°C increases by 13°C then temperature falls by 20°C.

Final temperature: _____

b 36°C falls by 17°C, then rises by 12°C, then falls by 15°C.

Final temperature: _____

c 5°C falls by 12°C, rises by 3°C, falls by 9°C, rises by 4°C and falls by 11°C.

Final temperature: _____ ⬤ 3

8 How long will it take these cars to travel 40 miles if their average speed is:

a 60 mph _____

b 32 mph _____

c 40 mph _____ ⬤ 3

9 Plum jam needs 600 g of sugar for every 750 g of plums. 300 ml of water is added to each kg of fruit, and the mixture has to boil until it reaches 104°C. 750 g of fruit makes 6 jars of jam.

If 3 kg of plums are to be made into jam:

a How many kg of sugar are needed? _____

b How many litres of water must be added? _____

c If the mixture is at 19°C, by how many degrees must the temperature increase during the cooking? _____

d How many jars of jam will be made? _____ ⬤ 4

4 Algebra

Letters are sometimes used in calculations instead of numbers.

Substitution questions are those where you are given the value for a letter, and then you substitute that value for the letter in the calculation and carry out the calculation.

REMEMBER!

When working with letters and numbers, remember that the $\times$ sign is not put between a number and a letter, so for example, $3b$ means $3 \times b$, and $4ab$ means $4 \times a \times b$.

Work out anything in brackets first of all, and then do any multiplication or division before any addition or subtraction.

Worked examples

1 What is the value of $2a + 57$ if $a = 5$?

   Substitute values for the letters: $(2 \times 5) + 57 = 10 + 57 = 67$

2 What is the value of $4b \div 3a$ if $b = 12$ and $a = 2$?

   Substitute values for the letters: $(4 \times 12) \div (3 \times 2) = 48 \div 6 = 8$

Equations can also use letters.

Remember that an equation is a little like a sentence. There are two parts, the first part being equal in value to the second part, with the two parts connected by the $=$ sign.

To solve an equation, that is, to find the value of an unknown letter, you need to work through these steps.

Collect all the terms with the unknown letter on one side of the equation. You do this by adding or subtracting, multiplying or dividing, to cancel out the term on one side. But whatever operation you do, you must do the same to both sides of the equation for the two parts to remain equal.

Worked example

$$5a + 4 = 3a + 20$$

To remove the $3a$ from the right-hand side, you must subtract $3a$. This must be done to *both* sides of the equation.

$$5a + 4 - 3a = 3a + 20 - 3a$$

This gives: $\quad\quad 2a + 4 = 20$

To get the term with the unknown letter on its own, you need to subtract 4 from the left side, so you must also subtract 4 from the right side.

$$2a + 4 - 4 = 20 - 4$$

This gives: $\quad\quad 2a = 16$

To get the value of a, divide both sides by 2.

This gives: $\quad\quad 2a \div 2 = 16 \div 2$

$$\text{So} \quad a = \mathbf{8}$$

Equations may also involve substitution, where there are two unknowns, and you are given the value for one of them and asked to determine the value of the other.

Worked example

If $7a + b \div 4 = 2a + 15 + 2b$, what is the value of a if b is 40?

Substitute the value for *b*: $\quad\quad 7a + 40 \div 4 = 2a + 15 + 80$

Subtract $2a$ from both sides of the equation to get all of the 'a' terms

on one side: $\quad\quad 7a + 10 - 2a = 2a + 15 + 80 - 2a$

This gives $\quad\quad 5a + 10 = 95$

Subtract 10 from both sides: $\quad\quad 5a + 10 - 10 = 95 - 10$

This gives: $\quad\quad 5a = 85$

Divide both sides by 5: $\quad\quad 5a \div 5 = 85 \div 5$

$$a = \mathbf{17}$$

Now it's your turn!

1 If $a = 7$ and $b = \frac{1}{4}$, what is the value of $20b - a$? _____ (7)

2 If $y = 25$ and $z = 17$, what is the value of $3z - 2y$? _____

3 What is the value of y if $3y + 13 = 49$? _____

4 If $3y^2 - 8 = 6^2 + 4$, $y =$ _____

5 If $4a + 13 = 6a - 9$, what is the value of a? _____

6 If $d = \frac{1}{2}$, $e = 5$ and $f = 3$, what is the value of $4def$? _____

7 $2x^2 + 8^2 - 5 = 91$, so $x =$ _____

8 If $S = \frac{1}{5}$, $T = \frac{1}{3}$ and $U = \frac{1}{2}$, what is the value of: **a** $18TU + 21 =$ _____ (3)

                                                         b $10S + 12T =$ _____

                                                         c $10^2 \div T + 14U =$ _____

How Did You Do?

In this section there were 10 marks available in the 'Now it's your turn!' exercise. Check your answers against the list on page 96. How many did you score?

- 7 or fewer correct? Work through the question types again and make sure that you fully understand each section. Once you have done this, try the questions again before you move on. If you had difficulty with any of the questions involving fractions, check back to section 1I for a reminder about operations with fractions.
- 8 correct or more. Well done! Do check any questions that were incorrect and make sure you understand where you made mistakes and why. See the end of Section 7 for some more algebra questions for you to try.

5 Linear sequences

Number sequences can take many forms. Here are some examples of the four most common types of sequence patterns you may come across in CEM and other 11+ exams.

1 A series with a constant difference between each term

   For example: 4, 8, 12, 16, 20, etc.   a difference of + 4 between each term

   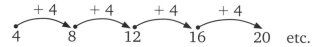
   4   8   12   16   20   etc.

2 A series with a regularly changing difference between each term

   For example: 1, 2, 4, 7, 11, 16, etc.   the difference between each term
                                                  increasing by 1 each time

   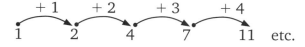
   1   2   4   7   11   etc.

3 A series made up of 'special' numbers

   For example: 1, 4, 9, 16, 25, etc.   square numbers

4 A series made up of two alternating series

   For example: **3**, 5, **6**, 7, **9**, 9, **12**, 11, **15**, etc.   the odd terms are a sequence
                                                                          increasing by 3

   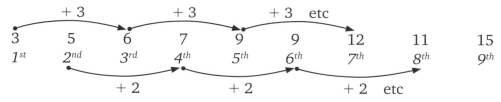
   3   5   6   7   9   9   12   11   15
   1st 2nd 3rd 4th 5th 6th 7th 8th 9th

                                                  the even terms are a sequence
                                                  increasing by 2 each time

If you cannot see the pattern straight away, try these strategies in turn until you find the solution.

Checklist

✓ Look carefully to see whether the sequence is made up of special numbers such as square, cube or triangular numbers.
✓ Write out the difference between each term as the pattern will often become clear.
✓ Write out the differences between alternate terms.

✓ PARENT TIP

Make up a rule to fit a telephone number sequence in any advert, then apply the rule to find the next 6 digits.

Worked examples

Find the next two terms in these sequences

1 17   20   25   32   41

Write in the differences between each term:

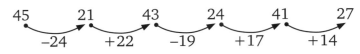

The difference is increasing by 2 each time.

So the next two terms are:

41 + 11 = **52**

52 + 13 = **65**

2 45   21   43   24   41   27

Look at the differences:

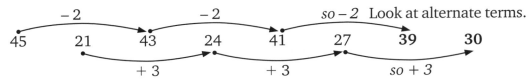

No obvious pattern?

so – 2 Look at alternate terms.

So the next two terms are **39** and **30**

Now it's your turn!

What number comes next in these sequences?   (10)

1 76, 75, 72, 67, 60, _____

2 350, 362, 374, 386, 398, _____

3 26, 19, 12, 5, –2, _____

4 1, 3, 6, 10, 15, _____

5 48, 34, 45, 39, 42, 44, 39, 49, _____

6 2016, 1008, 504, 252, _____

7 0.35, 0.49, 0.63, 0.77, _____

8 $\frac{1}{2}, \frac{2}{4}, \frac{3}{6}, \frac{4}{8},$ _____

9 99, 88, 78, 69, _____

10 2, 5, 10, 17, 26, _____

How Did You Do?

In this section there were 10 marks available in the 'Now it's your turn!' exercise. Check your answers against the list on page 96. How many did you score?

- 7 or fewer correct? Work through the question types again and make sure that you fully understand each type of sequence. Once you have done this, try the questions again before you move on.

- 8 correct or more. Well done! Do check any questions that were incorrect and make sure you understand where you made mistakes and why. See the end of Section 7 for some more linear sequence questions for you to try.

6 Problem solving

Tackling maths problems requires you to understand what you are being asked to work out and then, having extracted the relevant information, you need to work through the calculation carefully. Following each stage of the checklist below will ensure that you work systematically through any maths problem.

Don't jump to conclusions about what you think you have to do before you have read the question really carefully!

Checklist

- ☑ Read the question carefully!
- ☑ Read slowly 'out loud in your head' to make sure you don't skim over important words.
- ☑ Identify what you are being asked to do.
- ☑ Find the information you need from the question – drawing a diagram or chart may help.
- ☑ Check the units.
- ☑ Set out the calculation.
- ☑ Estimate your answer.
- ☑ Work through the calculation systematically.
- ☑ Check your answer – is it sensible? Is it the same order of magnitude at your estimate?

REMEMBER!

Mis-reading the question is still one of the most common errors made in test!

Worked example

A rectangular garden 20 m by 15 m is to have a path 1 metre wide all around the edge, and the rest to be grass.

REMEMBER!

A quick diagram will help you to see what happens at the corners!

If each path slab is 50 cm square, **i)** how many slabs will be needed and **ii)** what area will be grass?

Find **i)** the number of slabs and **ii)** the area of grass.

i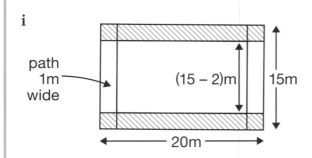

 2 × 20m × 1m

2 × (15 − 2)m × 1m

Notice that you must take away the corner square metres when calculating the short sides as they have

The path is made up of two 20 m long lengths and two (15 – 2) m short lengths, all 1 m wide.

So the area of the path is $(2 \times 20) + (2 \times 13) = 40 + 26 = 66$ square metres.

Each slab is 50 cm square, so 4 slabs are needed for 1 square metre.

So 66×4 slabs = **264 slabs needed**

    ii Area of lawn in square metres is $(15 – 2) \times (20 – 2)$

        Estimate less than 15×20 so < 300

        Calculation $(15 – 2) \times (20 – 2)$ $= 13 \times 18$

                                   $= (18 \times 3) + (18 \times 10)$

                                   $= 54 + 180$

Now it's your turn!

1 In a race, Tom's speed is 18 seconds. He is 2 seconds faster than Nathan but   (2)
3 seconds slower than Harry. Ted is 4 seconds ahead of Nathan.

    a What was Harry's time? _____   **b** Who was second? _____

2 One lorry load of gravel is needed to cover 50 square metres of a car park.   (1)
How many lorry loads will be needed for a car park 50 m long and 30 m wide?

_____

3 Tickets for a particular flight cost £376. A 5% saving can be made by booking   (1)
early. How much can be saved when buying four tickets if all four are booked

early? _____

4 A library has 21,000 books. At any one time $\frac{1}{3}$ of them are on loan and 1% of   (1)
the total stock are being repaired. Normally how many books are on the

shelves? _____

5 How many exercise books must a school order each term if every pupil needs   (1)
4 different exercise books, and there are 8 classes altogether. Half of the
classes have 30 children and the remaining classes have only $\frac{5}{6}$ of that number

of pupils. _____

6 Sandwiches are £2.40 each, small rolls are £1.80 and large rolls are £2.75. Tina   (1)
buys twice as many sandwiches as small rolls and just 1 large roll. If her change

from a £20 note is £4.05, how many sandwiches did she buy? _____

7 Ellie is 4 years older than Clare. Benji is 5 years younger than Ellie and 2 years   (1)

older than Sam. If Sam is 7 years old, how old is Clare? _____

8 A bath fills at the rate 7 litres per minute, and empties at the rate of 10 litres per   (1)
minute. How much longer does it take to fill bath tub with 35 litres than it takes

to empty it? _____

How Did You Do?

In this section there were 9 marks available in the 'Now it's your turn!' exercise. Check your answers against the list on page 96. How many did you score?

- 6 or fewer correct? Work through the question types again and make sure that you fully understand each section. Once you have done this, try the questions again before you move on.
- 7 correct or more. Well done! Do check any questions that were incorrect and make sure you understand where you made mistakes and why. See the end of Section 7 for some more problem solving questions for you to try.

7 Data and graphs

(A) *Data*

Data is the word that describes collections of information. The information may be words or numbers. Sets of data are often the result of making a series of measurements, for example children's hand spans, or the result of carrying out an investigation to answer a question, for example, what colour of car is most popular? Data sets also include timetables and records, such as sporting results or daily temperatures over time.

When data is collected, it is recorded in a table or chart. You may be asked to work with data by reading information from a table or chart. Descriptions about the distribution of the data that you are most likely to be asked to work out include the mean (the average), the median (the mid-point of the data set), the range (the spread of values in the data set) and the mode (the most common value). (The word 'average' is also used sometimes in place of 'mean'.)

Checklist

- ✓ To work out the mean of a set of data, you add together all the values and then divide by the total number of values.
- ✓ The median value of a set of data is the value that is at the mid-point between the highest and lowest value.
- ✓ The range of a set of data is the difference between the highest and the lowest value.
- ✓ The mode of a set of data is the most commonly occurring value.

Worked example

Identify the mean, median, range and mode of this set of test marks.

| 67 | 72 | 85 | 91 | 60 | 58 | 72 | 68 | 85 | 72 |

Mean = (67 + 72 + 85 + 91 + 60 + 58 + 72 + 68 + 85 + 72) ÷ 10
     = 730 ÷ 10 = **73**

For the next three, it helps to put the marks in order from least to greatest.

| 58 | 60 | 67 | 68 | 72 | | 72 | 72 | 85 | 85 | 91 |

Midway point is 72, so the median is **72**

Range   →   91 − 58 = **33**

Mode (most common score)   →   **72**

Now it's your turn!

1 A football team played six matches, with these results: (3)

Won   4 – 3   Won   3 – 1   Drew   3 – 3

Lost   3 – 5   Won   6 – 2   Won   5 – 4

   a What was the mean number of goals scored by the team? _____

   b What was the range of goals scored against them? _____

   c Considering all teams, what is the mode of the number of goals scored by any team? _____

2 Three children buy souvenirs. Caitlin spends £2.76, Toni spends £3.40 and Marie (1) spends £3.05. What was the average amount of money spent? _____

3 A shop sells the following numbers of pairs of shoes during a 10-day sale: (4)

No. of pairs each day: 13   7   20   7   3   10   12   8   11   9

   a How many pairs were sold altogether? _____

   b What was the range in the numbers of pairs sold each day? _____

   c What was the mean number of pairs sold per day? _____

   d What is the mode of the data? _____

(B) Graphs

Sets of data can also be represented in various graphs. A graph is a visual representation showing the connection between two things that vary.

The most frequently used types of graph use a horizontal axis (the x-axis), and a vertical axis the (y-axis).

Points on these graphs are identified using coordinates. Coordinates are given as a pair of numbers, with the value on the x axis given first, then the value on the y axis. In the graph below the coordinates for A are (3, 2).

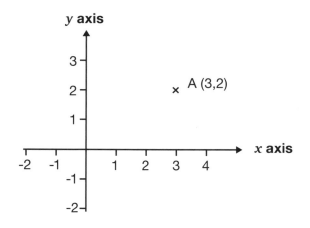

REMEMBER!

Remember that a graph can have positive and negative numbers!

The sections below show you the types of graphs and charts that you are most likely to come across in the CEM 11⁺ exams. You will need to be able to read information from the graphs as well as construct them from a given set of data. Remember to look carefully at any labels and in particular notice the scale and units used on each of the two axes.

Bar graph

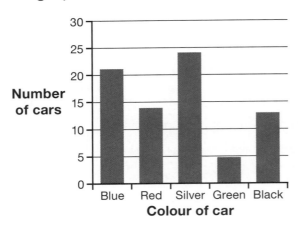

The axes of a bar graph must be labelled. Here the numbers on the *y*-axis indicate the number of cars, and each column is a different car colour. From this type of graph, it is very easy to see at a glance that the silver cars are most common and the green cars are the least common. Although the horizontal lines are only given for every 5 cars counted, it is easy to work out the in-between values, such as 21 blue cars and 14 red cars.

A bar graph is used when the categories along the *x*-axis are distinct (or discrete), such as colour, shoe size or name.

REMEMBER!

When constructing your own bar graph, remember to choose a sensible scale for the two axes and label them clearly.

Line graph

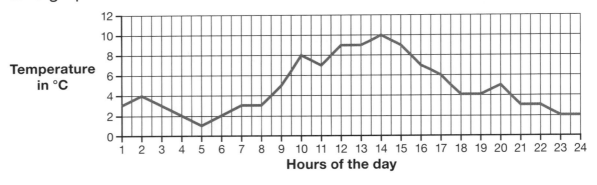

A line graph is good for showing trends. From this graph of temperature through the day, you can easily see that the temperature generally rises during the day and falls at night. You can read the temperature at any particular time from this graph by following up the vertical line from each hour and then look across to the *y*-axis to work out the value of the point on the plotted line.

A line graph is used when the variable along the *x*-axis is a continuous variable, rather than separate items.

Individual values are written against the vertical lines along the *x*-axis, rather than in the spaces as with a bar graph.

Tally chart

If a set of data is made up of a number of individual items or occurrences which are collected by direct observation, a tally chart is a very useful way of collecting the data. It is just a quick way of keeping count. One tally – a short vertical line – is made for each item, event or occurrence.

| || ||| |||| ┼┼┼┼

Every 5th one is recorded by adding a horizontal line through the previous 4 vertical lines. At the end totals can be found quicklyby adding up the groups of five.

For practice see how quickly you can total these tallies:

┼┼┼┼ ┼┼┼┼ ||| —————

┼┼┼┼ ┼┼┼┼ ┼┼┼┼ ┼┼┼┼ | —————

┼┼┼┼ ┼┼┼┼ ┼┼┼┼ ┼┼┼┼ ┼┼┼┼ ┼┼┼┼ || —————

┼┼┼┼ ┼┼┼┼ ┼┼┼┼ ┼┼┼┼ ┼┼┼┼ ┼┼┼┼ —————

Scatter graph

Sometimes sets of data are made up of separate pairs of measurements, such as age and height or waist and height. These data can be plotted on a graph with one axis for each of the variables, and each item is indicated by one point on the graph. The points are not joined up as they are not linked to each other in any way. Once a number of points have been plotted a pattern may emerge. This might show that the measure on the y axis generally increases as the measure on the x axis increases:

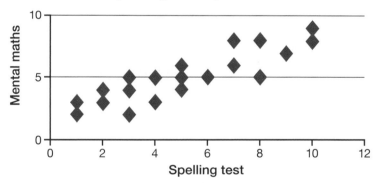

Or it may be the opposite, with the measure on the y-axis decreasing as the measure on the x-axis increases:

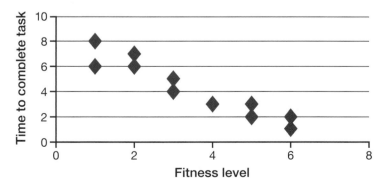

The points are unlikely to lie in a straight line but they may show a trend or general pattern. If the points seem to be randomly distributed across the graph then there is no connection or correlation between the two variables being plotted.

Pictogram

A pictogram uses a picture or symbol to represent a certain number on a graph.

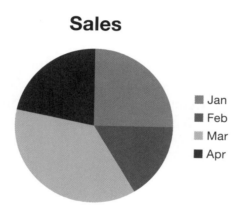

Month	April	May	June	July
				☺
				☺
		☺		☺
		☺	☺	☺
	☺	☺	☺	☺
	☺	☺	☺	☺
	☺	☺	☺	☺
	☺	☺	☺	☺

Number of people in the park

☺ = 50 people

Pictograms can sometimes use half of a symbol to represent half of the amount, so in this example half of a smiley face would represent 25 people.

Pie chart

Sales

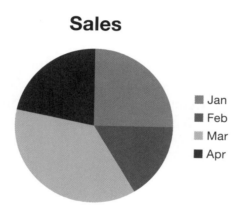

- ■ Jan
- ■ Feb
- ■ Mar
- ■ Apr

A pie chart is a circle divided into sections, or slices, the angle or size of which shows the relative proportions of different groups or categories.

In CEM 11⁺ type exams, you need to know how to interpret pie charts, working out the sizes of sections and understanding what they represent.

In a pie chart the 360° of the circle are shared between the total number of items being represented. In this example, it is the total sales divided into four months; January, February, March and April.

From this diagram, you can easily rank the months in terms of sales, and see that March has the greatest number as it is the largest sector.

Numbers of sales can be calculated if the angle of the sector is known. In this diagram, January sales occupy one quarter of the circle (it has a right angle in the centre, indicating that it is one quarter of the circle).

✔ PARENT TIP

When serving up a cake, pie or pizza, talk about the angles and numbers of slices in the whole.

If the total number of sales is 1000, the sales for January will be 1000 ÷ 4 = 250.

Venn diagram

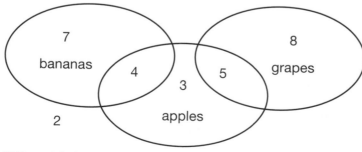

Different fruit preferred by a class of children

A Venn diagram is a series of overlapping circles, with each circle representing a different category. The members, or number of members, of each category are listed within the appropriate circle.

Members of more than one category are written in the overlapping sections, and members that do not belong to any category or group are written outside of the set of circles.

In the example above, the different groups are identified and the numbers in each category are recorded in this table.

Only like bananas	7
Only like grapes	8
Only like apples	3
Don't like apples, bananas or grapes	2
Like apples and bananas	4
Like apple and grapes	5

Now it's your turn!

4 This graph shows the number of books read in the holidays by a group of children.   (3)

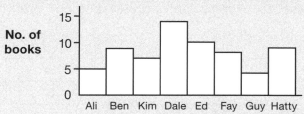

Graph to show number of books read in holidays

a Who read the most books? _____

b The target was to read at least five books. Who did not meet the target? _____

c What is the mode of this set of data? _____

5   (3)

TRAIN

PLANE

5

4

6

2

1

0

3

FERRY

Different forms of transport taken on holiday

a How many children took a plane and a train only? _____

b Which was the most commonly used form of transport? _____

c How many children used just one form of transport? _____

6 A group of children recorded the types of vehicles passing ther school in one hour. (3)

Car	ⅢⅢ ⅢⅢ ⅢⅢ ⅢⅢ ⅢⅢ IIII
Lorry	ⅢⅢ ⅢⅢ II
Van	ⅢⅢ ⅢⅢ ⅢⅢ III
Bus	ⅢⅢ I
Bike	ⅢⅢ ⅢⅢ

a How many vehicles of any sort were recorded? _____

b What fraction were bikes? _____

c What percentage were vans? _____

How Did You Do?

In this section there were 17 marks available in the 'Now it's your turn!' exercises. Check your answers against the list on page 96. How many did you score?

- 13 or fewer correct? Work through the question types again and make sure that you fully understand each section. Once you have done this, try the questions again before you move on.
- 14 correct or more. Well done! Do check any questions that were incorrect and make sure you understand where you made mistakes and why. Here is a test with some more data and graph questions for you to try. Please note the test also contains questions on algebra, sequences and problem solving.

Algebra, linear sequences, problem solving and data and graphs test

1 This chart records the minimum and maximum temperatures for five days.

Temp in °C	Day 1	Day 2	Day 3	Day 4	Day 5
Maximum	24	18	7	10	26
Minimum	16	13	−4	−1	13

a By how many degrees did the temperature fall on the hottest day? _____

b On which day/s did the temperature fall below freezing?

_____

c On which day was there the smallest difference between the maximum and minimum temperatures? _____

d If these 5 days are taken to represent the year, what is the average temperature difference between the maximum and minimum?

_____   4

2 What is the value of x in these equations?

a $5x + 23 = 58$ $x =$ _____

b $2x^2 - 17 = 55$ $x =$ _____

c $2x + 14 = 5x - 52$ $x =$ _____

d $8x \div 4 + 12 = 5x - 9$ $x =$ _____

e $22x - 33 = 11x$ $x =$ _____   3

3 Parcel A is 400 g heavier than parcel B, and 50 g lighter than parcel D. Parcel C is 150 g heavier than parcel D. If parcel B is 400 g, what is the mass of parcel C? _____   1

4 Give the next 2 terms in each of these sequences.

a 171, 170, 168, 165, 161, _____ _____

b 21, 2, 18, 5, 15, 8, 12, 11, _____ _____

c 1.75, 3.00, 4.25, 5.50, _____ _____

d 1, 1, 2, 3, 5, 8, _____ _____

e $13\frac{1}{3}$, $11\frac{2}{3}$, 10, $8\frac{1}{3}$, _____ _____   5

5 Adam is 2 years older than Tom, and 5 years younger than Ali. Ben is 12 years old. He is 4 years older than Ali. How old is Tom?

_____

6 Craig spends £21.63 at the supermarket. One-third of the amount was spent on items that were half price. What would his total bill have been

had all the goods been bought at full price? _____

7 This graph shows the hand span of a group of children in relation to their shoe size.

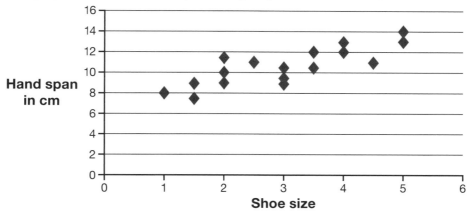

From the information given in this graph, which of the following statements are true and which are false?

A shoe size of 2 always has a hand span greater than 10 cm.   TRUE / FALSE

There is no connection between shoe size and hand span.   TRUE / FALSE

The person with the smallest shoe size has the smallest hand span. TRUE / FALSE

Hand spans always increase as shoe size increases.   TRUE / FALSE

Generally children with larger shoe sizes have larger hand spans.   TRUE / FALSE

8 A postman has 160 houses on his round and normally has deliveries for 90% of them each day. During one 5 day week he delivered 2160 letters. What was the average number of letters per house per day that week?

_____

9 The data from a minibeast survey is shown on this tally chart. Present it as a graph on the grid below. Label the axes, then answer the questions.

Caterpillars	┼┼┼┼ ┼┼┼┼ ┼┼┼┼ ┼┼┼┼ ┼┼┼┼ ┼┼┼┼ ┼┼┼┼ ┼┼┼┼ ‖‖‖
Woodlice	┼┼┼┼ ┼┼┼┼ ┼┼┼┼ ┼┼┼┼ ‖‖
Worms	┼┼┼┼ ┼┼┼┼ ‖
Snails	┼┼┼┼ ‖‖
Beetles	┼┼┼┼ ┼┼┼┼ ‖‖‖

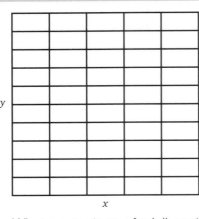

y

x

a What percentage of minibeasts were beetles? _____

b How many more woodlice than snails? _____

c If the caterpillars were all found on 4 cabbage plants, how many

caterpillars on average on each plant? _____ ◯ 3

10 A car travels from A to B at 30 mph. It takes 4 hours to reach B. Leaving at the same time and on the same route, a car travels from B to A at 60 mph. If they both depart at 10:00, at what time will they pass each other?

_____

11 In a jar of 200 coloured sweets, 5% are red, $\frac{1}{5}$th are green, 30 are yellow and the rest are an equal mixture of orange and plain. How many orange

sweets are there in the jar? _____ ◯ 2

12 If $a = 7$, $b = 0.5$ and $c = 11$, what is the value of:

a $3c - 2a =$ _____

b $4ab + 2c =$ _____

c $c^2 - a^2 =$ _____

d $(4c) \div b =$ _____

e $5bc$ _____ ◯ 5

13 This pie chart shows the popularity of different flavours of ice cream

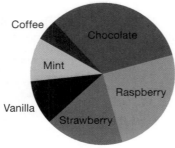

a Which flavour was the least popular? _____

b Which two flavours were equally popular? _____

c If 240 people were asked, how many chose raspberry? _____

◯ 3

Key non-verbal reasoning skills

(A1) Similarities

Questions requiring you to look for similarities between shapes and patterns can be asked in lots of different ways. For example:

'Which one on the right is most similar to the ones on the left?'

or 'Which one on the right belongs to the group on the left?'

When expressed in this sort of way, the question will give some shapes or patterns at the beginning of the line. Very often, three shapes or patterns are given though it can be more and occasionally will be just two. However many patterns are given, the same method applies.

1 Look carefully at the given shapes.
2 Identify the features that they all have in common – it is often helpful to eliminate obvious features that they do *not* share first of all.
3 Then look along the answer options.
4 Cross out any of the options that do not have the common features.
5 If more than one answer option looks possible, look again at the beginning of the line to identify further details.
6 Apply this more detailed information to the possible answers to arrive at the one that is most similar.

Worked example

          a   b   c   d   e

What do the stars in the group at the beginning of the line have in common?

Shape?	all stars	so must be a star
Size?	all different sizes	can be any size
Shading?	all different	can be any shading
Orientation?	some straight, some angled	can be any orientation
Number of points?	all have 5	so must have 5 points

They are all stars with 5 points.

Now look along the answer options – ignore size, shading and orientation.

Shape?   all are stars

Number of points?   a has 4   b has 5   c has 6   d has 7   e has 4

Therefore **option b**, the **star** with **5 points**, is the answer.

Questions asking 'Which is the odd one out?' require the same approach.

In these questions, there is a row of shapes and again you need to identify all the features they have in common.

Work systematically through the features until you find one that occurs in all but one of the options. This then indicates the odd one out.

> **✔ PARENT TIP**
>
> *Doing 'Spot the difference' puzzles improves observational skills.*

Worked example

| a | b | c | d | e |

Shape?	all quadrilaterals
Right angles?	present in c and e
Parallel lines?	2 pairs in b, c and e, 1 pair in a and d
Outline?	solid black line on all
Symmetrical?	all have at least 1 line of symmetry, b, c and e have more
Shading?	all have oblique lines
Angle of shading lines?	top left to lower right in a, b, c and e,

not d, which is lower left to top right

so **option d** is the odd one out

Now it's your turn!

Which one on the right belongs to the group on the left? (2)

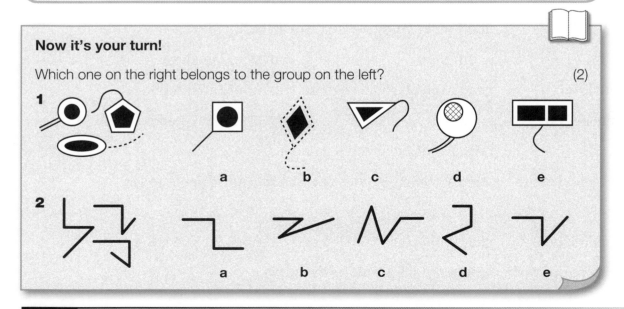

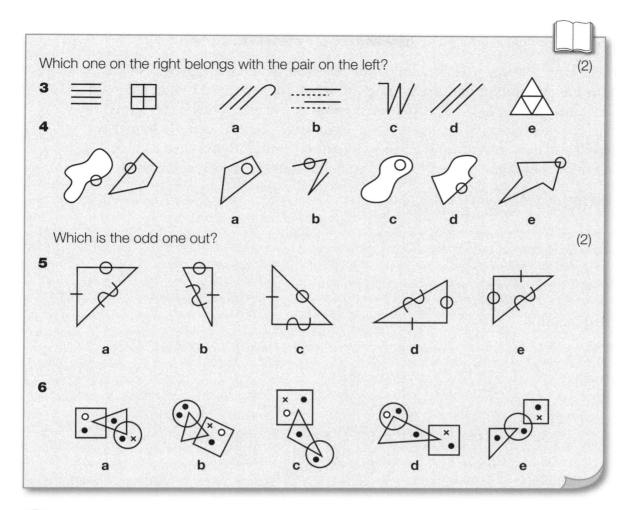

Which one on the right belongs with the pair on the left? (2)

3

4

Which is the odd one out? (2)

5

6

B2 Analogies

An analogy is the comparison of one pair of words, objects or patterns with another pair. Verbal reasoning tests have these types of questions using words. In non-verbal reasoning questions, the pairs are of pictures, shapes or patterns.

Questions of this sort require you to look at the first given pair. Identify how the two parts of the pair are connected or related, then apply that same connection to complete the second pair.

The instruction for these questions will be something like:

'Which pattern completes the second pair in the same way as the first pair?'

To find the answer, you have to identify within the first pair:

1 Which elements of the first pattern have stayed the same in the second pattern?
2 Which elements of the first pattern have changed?
3 How have the elements that have changed been changed?

Then look carefully at the second pair.

The element(s) or characteristic(s) that were the same in the first pair must remain the same in the second pair.

This might be shape, size, shading, number, orientation and so on. Identify this element, or elements, in the first of the two patterns in the second pair and then cross out any answer options without the element(s) or characteristic(s).

The element(s) or characteristic(s) that changed are applied to the second pair.

Again this might be shape, size, shading, number, orientation or another variable. Look at the answer options and cross out any that have not changed in the same way as the first pair, which will leave the correct answer. If it seems that you are left with more than one possible answer, inspect them both very carefully. Identify how they are different and then go back to the first pair to find how this detail changed (or remained the same) in the first pair to help you eliminate the incorrect answer.

 **PARENT TIP**

Looking carefully at shapes and patterns when completing jigsaw puzzles practises the skills needed for these questions.

Worked example

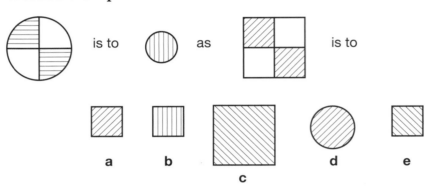

1 Which elements of the first pattern have stayed the same in the second pattern?

   same shape, some shading

2 Which parts of the first pattern have changed?

   size, divisions, shading style

3 How have the parts that have changed been changed? .

   smaller, not in quarters, whole shape shaded not just two quarters, angle of shading lines

Looking at the second pair, there is a large square in quarters with two quarters shaded with diagonal lines.

Staying the same?	Shape – square so not option d
	Shading – diagonal lines so not option b
Changes?	Smaller size – not option c
	Not divided into quarters – none to cross off
	Angle of shading lines – diagonal to be top left to bottom right so not option a
	Option e is the correct answer.

Now it's your turn!

Which pattern completes the second pair in the same way as the first pair?

(3)

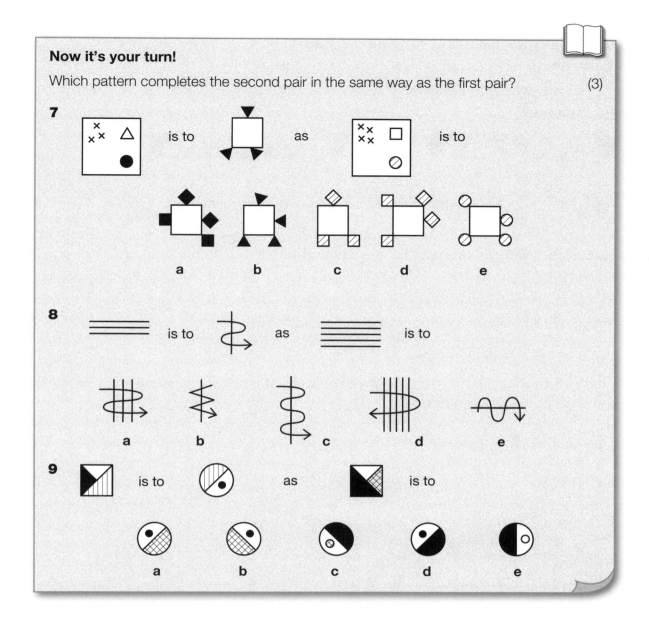

C3 Sequences and grids

Sequences

As with number sequences, in non-verbal reasoning the terms may be in a simple step-by-step progression. In these, you have to identify the pattern between the terms to work out the one that comes next.

Worked example

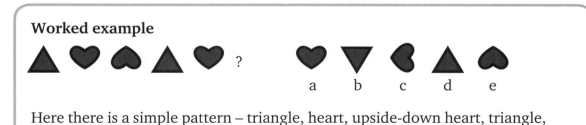

Here there is a simple pattern – triangle, heart, upside-down heart, triangle, heart and so on.

So the next term is an upside-down heart, which is **option e**.

More often the sequence has two or more progressions happening. In this example, you need to notice the shape of the terms, their orientation and the shading.

Things to look out for in sequences:

Checklist

- ✓ Shape
- ✓ Number of sides or angles
- ✓ Types of angles, e.g. right angles
- ✓ Orientation of shape
- ✓ Position of different elements, e.g. top or bottom, inside or outside
- ✓ Size variations
- ✓ Shading patterns

Now it's your turn!

Which picture or pattern on the bottom row comes next in the pattern on the top row?

(3)

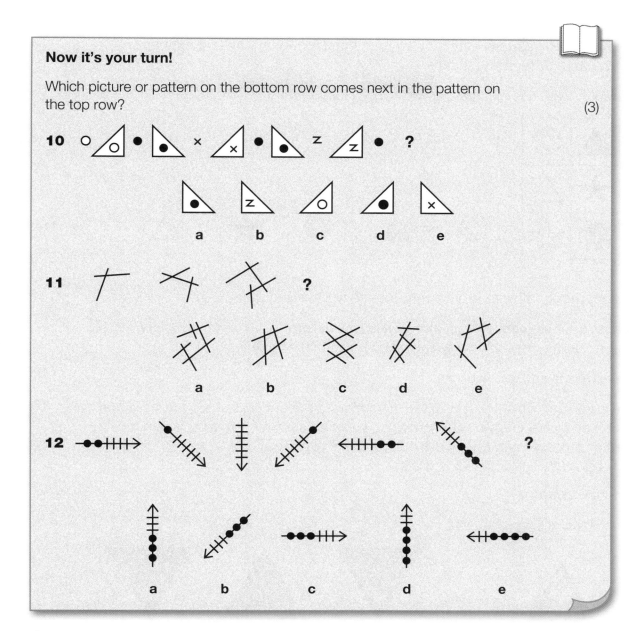

Grids

Identifying the missing patterns in a grid uses the skills associated with other non-verbal reasoning question types generally, and often specifically includes sequences or analogies.

Remember that a sequence or pattern may progress along a grid, moving from left to right in every row:

→ → →

→ → →

→ → →

Alternatively, it may 'snake' its way down:

→ → →

← ← ←

→ → →

The pattern may be in columns or rows, or both.

One element of the pattern may follow one sequence and another element may follow a second, different sequence.

For example: Which is the missing pattern?

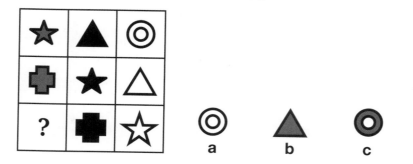

In this grid, the shading style is by column – so the missing shape is grey.

The shapes are a sequence going along each row in turn – that is star, triangle, circle, cross, star, triangle and so on – so the missing shape is a circle.

The grey circle is answer **option c.**

In some grids, the central part is made up of elements from each surrounding shape. By looking at each section carefully in turn, you can identify the part that is removed, reflected or repeated and then work out the missing pattern.

Worked example

Which is the missing pattern?

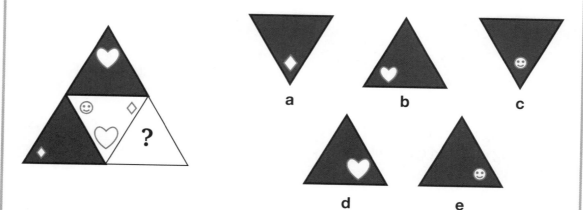

The pattern in each corner of the central triangle is repeated in the outer triangle, and in the missing section it will be the smiley face.

The pattern is in the outer corner (angle) of the opposite triangle so **option e** is the correct answer.

Now it's your turn!

Which is the missing pattern?

(5)

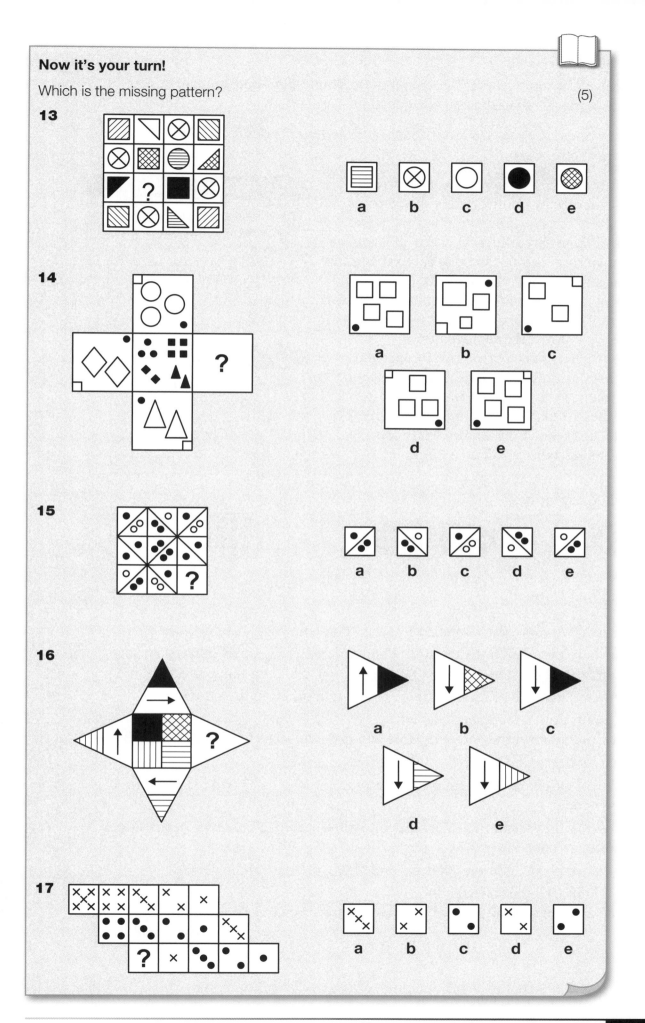

D4 Codes

Codes can seem complicated! But follow these simple steps and you will be able to crack any non-verbal reasoning code question.

Code questions may use two-letter codes or three-letter codes. You follow the same process for both.

1 Identify which feature is represented by the letters in turn by finding two of the patterns that share the same first letter in their code.
2 Look at them carefully, asking the question 'In what way are they the same as each other and different from the other patterns?'
3 Look at the other patterns with different first letters. You would expect them all to have different types of the same feature.
4 Note which type is represented by each letter in the first position of the code, and so work out the first code letter for the unknown pattern.

Repeat these steps (1–4) for the second letter of the code, and again for the third letter of a three-lettered code question.

Worked example

AX   BY   CX   AZ
(1)   (2)   (3)   (4)   ?

1 Which two share the same first letter in their code?   (1) and (4) are both A

2 How are they similar to each other and different from the other patterns?   Arrow shape pointing in same direction

3 Others start with different letters and point in different directions.

4 B points down, C points to the left.
 The unknown at the end of the line points down, so its first letter will be B.

Repeat for the second letter:

1 Which two share the same second letter in their code?   (1) and (3) are both X

2 How are they similar to each other and different from the other patterns?   Same type of shading

3 Others start with different letters and have different shading styles.

4 Y is white, Z is a squared pattern
 The unknown at the end has a squared pattern, so its second letter is Z.

                                             Answer: BZ

Now it's your turn!

Which code matches the shape or pattern at the end of each line? (3)

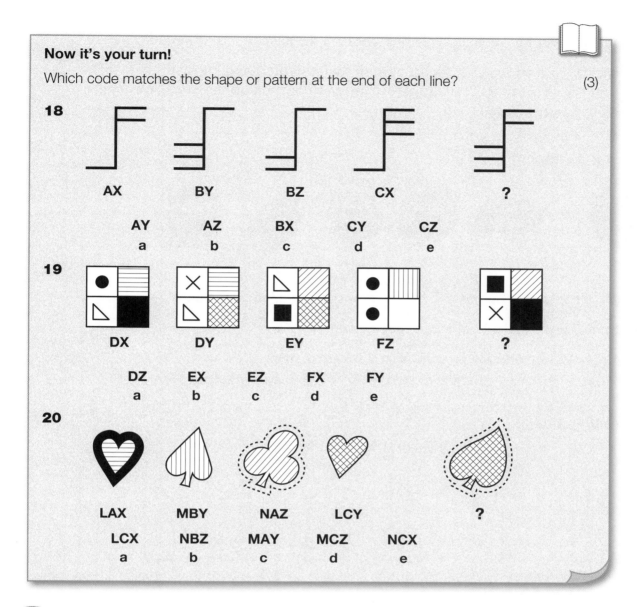

18   AX   BY   BZ   CX   ?

AY   AZ   BX   CY   CZ
a   b   c   d   e

19   DX   DY   EY   FZ   ?

DZ   EX   EZ   FX   FY
a   b   c   d   e

20   LAX   MBY   NAZ   LCY   ?

LCX   NBZ   MAY   MCZ   NCX
a   b   c   d   e

E5 Reflections and rotations

Some non-verbal reasoning questions require you to identify the reflection of a shape, usually giving you the mirror line in which the shape is reflected. This mirror line is also a line of symmetry between the shape and its reflection.

Worked example

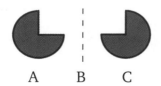

A   B   C

A is the given image, B is the line of reflection or mirror line, and C is the image reflected in that line.

Shapes may also be rotated. They will be identical to the original shape, not 'flipped over' as in a mirror image, but their orientation on the page will be different.

Questions may ask you to identify the pattern that is a rotation of the pattern given. Remember the shape must be identical but just in a different orientation. Do not get confused by a mirror image!

Worked example

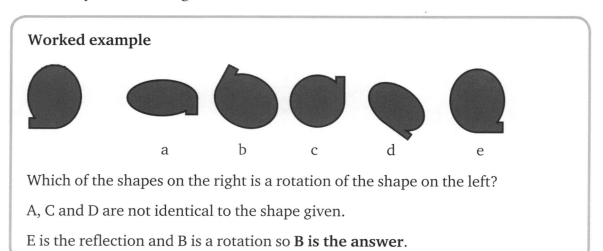

Which of the shapes on the right is a rotation of the shape on the left?

A, C and D are not identical to the shape given.

E is the reflection and B is a rotation so **B is the answer**.

Now it's your turn!

Which pattern on the right is a reflection of the one on the left? (3)

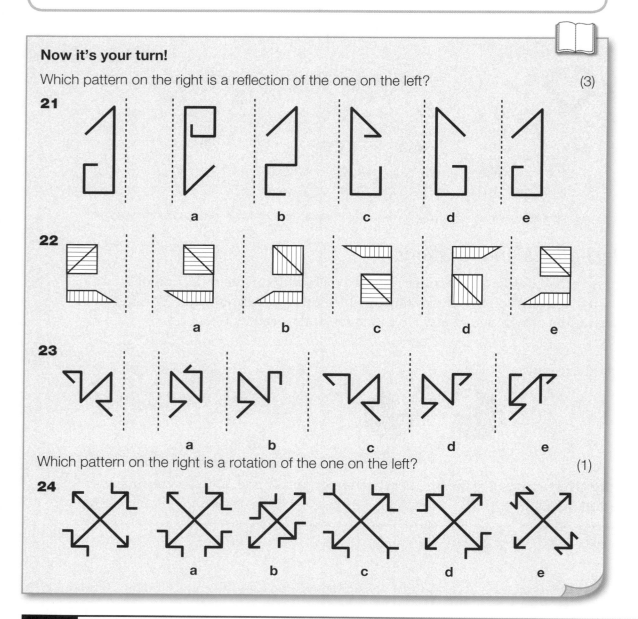

Which pattern on the right is a rotation of the one on the left? (1)

Non-verbal reasoning tests often include questions requiring you to identify which cube can, or cannot, be made from a given net.

 REMEMBER!

First read the question carefully to see if you are looking for the cube that *can* be made or the cube that *can't* be made!

To do these questions, you need to be able to visualise the 3-D shape and relate the different faces to the different positions on the net.

✔ **PARENT TIP**

Draw and cut out the net of a cube. Add a simple design or character on each face. Fold up. Inspect which squares from the net end up next to each other. Notice the orientation of any shape or pattern when folded, then unfold to see the position on the net.

Some helpful hints:

Look at the direction of any specific shape such as an arrow and notice to which adjacent square/face it is pointing.

Three patterns in a row on the net cannot be observed from one side on a cube.

Patterns on opposite faces will not be observed.

Look at this example: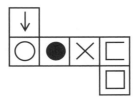

- The arrow is pointing towards the white circle so on any cube which shows the arrow check to see whether it is pointing to the white circle.

- The white circle, black circle and X are all in a line, therefore they cannot all be seen at one time in any cube. This applies to any three faces which are in a line on the net.

- Notice the orientation of any diagonal line or shape with respect to the faces adjacent to it – these need to be checked out on the cube images.

Worked example

Which cube cannot be made from the given net?

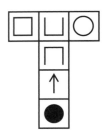

           a   b   c   d   e

Check for the pairs of patterns that cannot be on adjacent faces:

Square cannot be next to a white circle	none have this
Arrow cannot point to the side or top of the U shape	none have this
Black circle cannot be next to the top of a U shape	none have this
The two U shapes cannot be in different orientations if adjacent	option d has the U shapes facing different ways so the cube in **option d** cannot be made from this net

Now it's your turn!

Which cube cannot be made from these nets? (2)

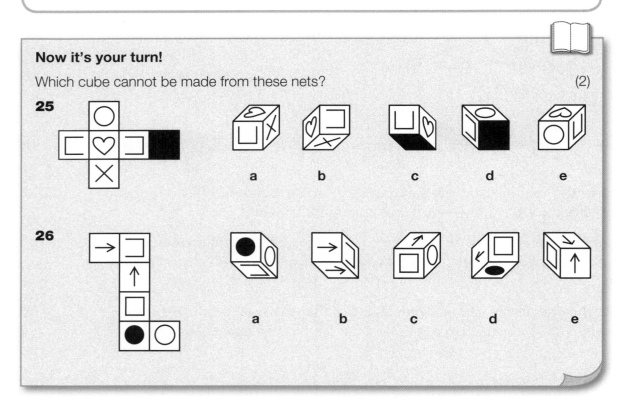

82   **CEM How To Do Maths and Non-verbal Reasoning**

Which cube can be made from the given net? (2)

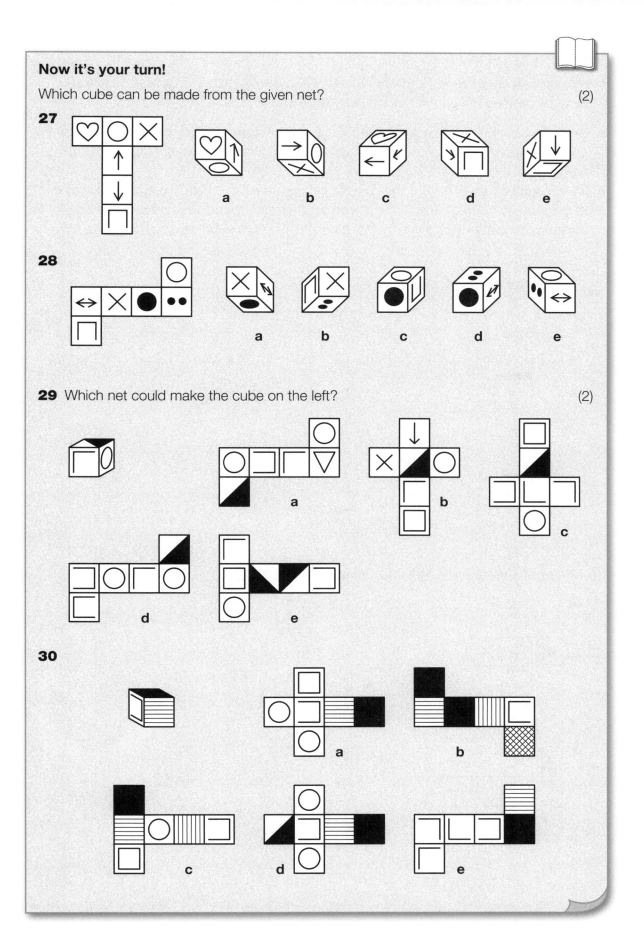

27

28

29 Which net could make the cube on the left? (2)

30

How Did You Do?

In this section there were 30 marks available in the 'Now it's your turn!' exercise. Check your answers against the list on page 95. How many did you score?

- 24 or fewer correct? Work through the question types again and make sure that you fully understand each section. Once you have done this, try the questions again before you move on.
- 25 correct or more. Well done! Do check any questions that were incorrect and make sure you understand where you made mistakes and why. Here is a non-verbal reasoning test with a mixture of question types for you to try.

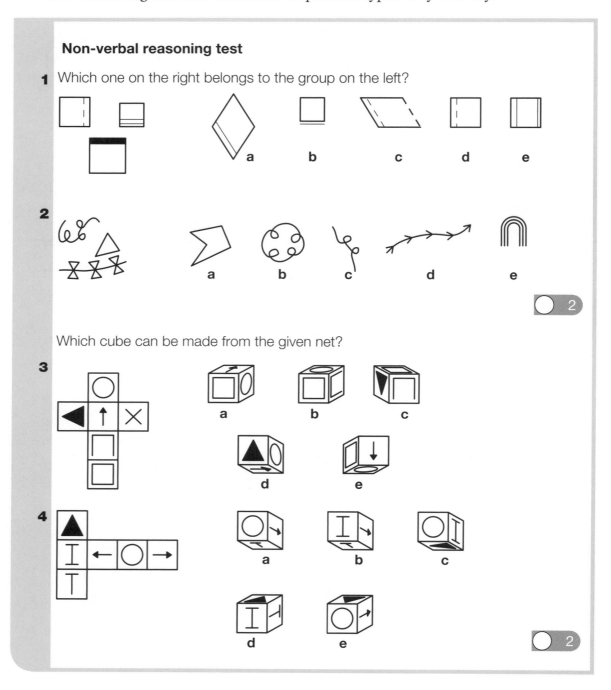

Non-verbal reasoning test

1 Which one on the right belongs to the group on the left?

a   b   c   d   e

2

a   b   c   d   e

Which cube can be made from the given net?

3

a   b   c

d   e

4

a   b   c

d   e

Which one comes next?

5

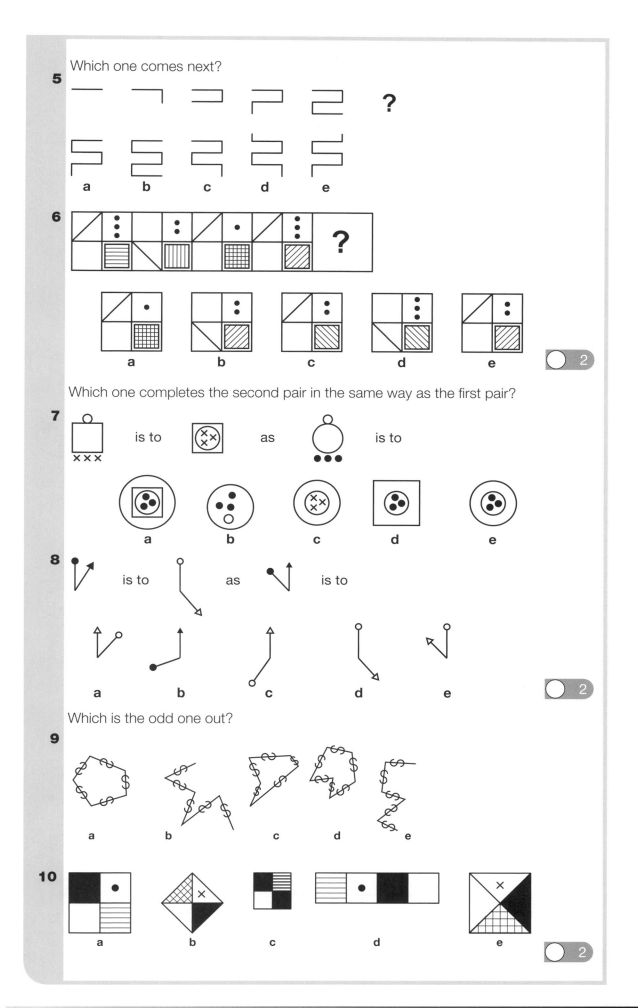

a   b   c   d   e

6

?

a   b   c   d   e

2

Which one completes the second pair in the same way as the first pair?

7

is to   as   is to

a   b   c   d   e

8

is to   as   is to

a   b   c   d   e

2

Which is the odd one out?

9

a   b   c   d   e

10

a   b   c   d   e

2

Which code matches the one at the end?

11

AX	BX	CY	AZ	?
BZ	CZ	AY	BY	CX
a	**b**	**c**	**d**	**e**

12

ALR	BMR	CLS	?	
CNS	ANR	BLT	AMS	CMT
a	**b**	**c**	**d**	**e**

Which cube cannot be made from the net?

13

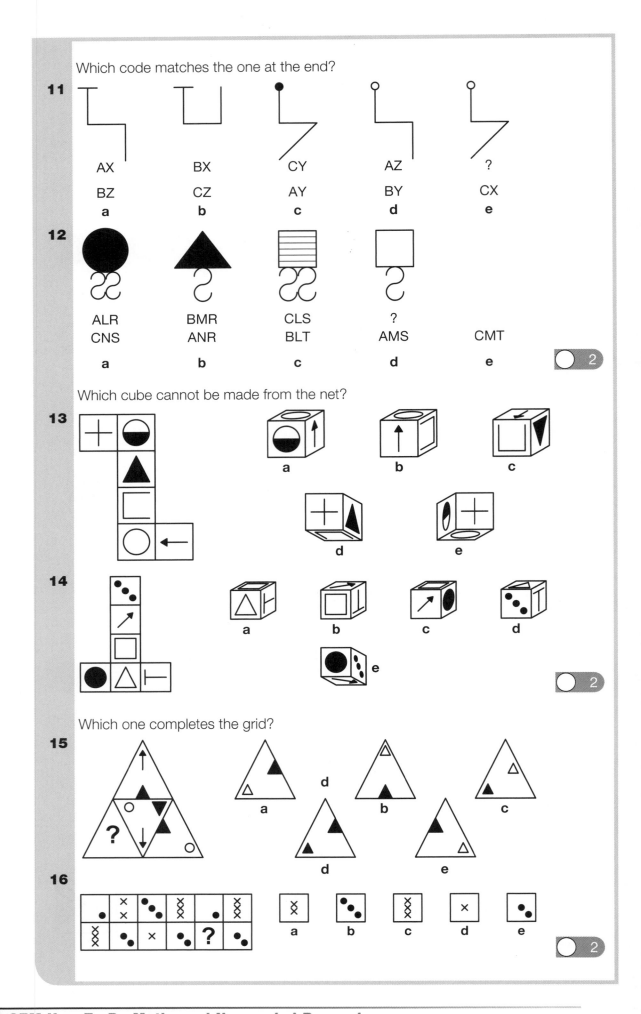

a   b   c

d   e

14

a   b   c   d

e

Which one completes the grid?

15

a   d   b   c

d   e

16

a   b   c   d   e

Which one is a reflection of the one on the left?

17

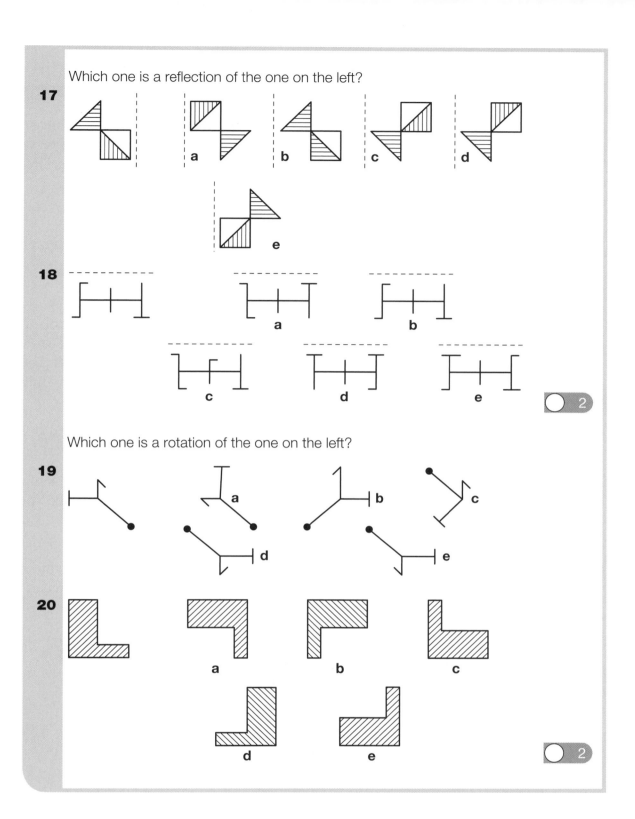

18

Which one is a rotation of the one on the left?

19

20

2

How do you prepare for the exam?

With the CEM exam, there is an emphasis on speed and you may not be able to complete the whole paper. Questions may also be presented in different ways. It is important therefore not to panic, but to read any instructions really carefully and then work quickly and methodically through each section.

Here are some tips to help with this:

1 Read each question carefully so that you know what to do – don't be tempted to skim-read the first time and then guess what you have to do.

2 Focus on what each question is asking you to do.

3 Use a watch, clock or timer when you are practising at home so that you get used to what 5 minutes feels like or what 10 minutes feels like, so that you can manage your time well. The *Bond Ten Minute Tests* will certainly help with this. The *Bond CEM 11+ Test Papers* are also broken up into timed sections, which you might find useful.

4 Use any opportunity at home to practise core number skills such as multiplication tables and number bonds – remember you need to be fast and accurate!

5 There are many different ways of presenting maths problems and reasoning questions, but the basic techniques and methods that you have learned and practised will enable you to tackle them confidently. So don't panic if the question 'looks' different.

6 Never, ever, sit at the end of any section of the exam and wonder what to do. Use every single second to check properly. Redo as many questions as you can to fill in the time. If you are capable of scoring 100 per cent, it would be a shame to miss a mark because you didn't spot the mistake.

REMEMBER!

As with every exam, make sure that you check through your paper and take an educated guess at anything that you don't know. Always use the full amount of time to double-check and, if possible, to work through some of the questions again to check that your answer is correct.

Effective checking

We always ask you to check carefully but you may not have been shown how to. Here are some tips to help:

• If you have finished a section, check that you have put an answer for every single question.

- An educated guess is better than a pure luck guess so try to eliminate any of the options. This gives you the best chance at getting your guess correct.

- Are your answers sensible? Do they show the correct units where needed?

- If all else fails and you cannot eliminate anything at all, then a 'pure luck' guess is better than nothing at all, so try not to leave any blanks at all if you possibly can.

- If you have time and you have already checked that every question has an answer, now work out which of the questions you found trickiest. Go back to them and redo them to see whether you get the same answer. If so, move on to the next trickiest until you either run out of time, or you find a question that gives you a different answer. If you do find a different answer, work out the question again to give you a third possible answer. You hope that the third will match either your first or second attempt. If not, try again until you find a matching answer.

- If you have completed all of your answers and you have managed to work through all of them for a second time, then you have done a thorough check.

- Don't assume that looking at your working out will find the right answer. Always go back to the actual question and begin again from the start as your working out might be problematic.

How to deal with different formats

The types of questions covered here are likely to be similar to those that you'll find in the CEM exam. Many will hopefully be identical but there is always the element of change. This is because the exam board are trying to test how you think, and not whether you can solve a specific type of question. Here is a successful technique to help you with this:

If you place your hand into a 'thumbs up' position we are going to start with the little finger and ask our way up the hand until we reach a 'thumbs up' like this:

4 Is the answer reasonable?

3 What process do I need to follow?

2 What information is given?

1 What is the question asking me to find?

1 What is the question asking me to find?

For example, am I being asked to solve an equation, carry out a multiplication, calculate an area, estimate a measurement, complete a sequence, crack a code or find the odd one out? Be clear in your mind what it is you have to do.

2 What information is given?

For example, numbers, measurements, angles, costs, frequencies, times or a group of shapes or sequence of patterns. Identify what information you need and find it in the question. If the information doesn't appear to be there, how can I use the information given to get the information that I need?

3 What process do I need to follow?

Does it remind me of a question type that I have a technique for, or is it similar to a technique I have already used? If not, can I find a strategy that would work to solve this problem? With non-verbal reasoning questions remember to consider shape, size, shading, position and number as you work out the solution.

4 Is the answer reasonable?

With maths questions do check that any answer you have got is reasonable, sensible and expressed in the correct units.

GOOD LUCK!

 **REMEMBER!**

You aren't going to be asked to do the impossible, so think about the skills, techniques and knowledge that you already have and try problem solving with these tools. The answer is often far easier than you first thought!

 **PARENT TIP**

The more problem solving your child does, the easier it is to think in different ways. Board games or computer games of strategy are useful, as are puzzle books that have a range of 'brain training' strategies.

Glossary

< sign meaning 'is less than'

> sign meaning 'is greater than'

area the surface of a shape measured in square units, e.g. square centimetres, which can be written as cm²

average the average is found by totalling a number of values and dividing by the number of values added together

clockwise moving round a circle or a point in the direction of the hands of the clock

coordinate a coordinate is a pair of numbers used to locate a point. The first number is the distance along the horizontal line and the second number is the distance along the vertical line.

cube a cube is a regular 3-D solid shape where every face is an identical square and every angle is a right angle.

cubic centimetre the volume of a cube that is 1 cm wide, 1 cm deep and 1 cm high

cubic metre the volume of a cube that is 1 m wide, 1 m deep and 1 m high

cuboid a 3-D solid shape where each surface is a rectangle (includes squares) and every angle is a right angle

cylinder a 3-D solid with two flat circular faces joined by one curved surface

decimal common way to refer to a number that has parts less than one that are expressed using a decimal point, for example a half is 0.5

degrees (1) the unit of measurement for temperature (2) the unit of measurement of angles, with 360 degrees making one complete turn

diameter the distance across a circle passing through the centre

difference to find the difference between two numbers, take the smaller number away from the larger number

digit a digit is any of the numerals 0, 1, 2, 3, 4, 5, 6, 7, 8 or 9

dozen 12

edge the edge of a solid shape is the line along which two adjacent faces meet

equivalent fractions fractions written with different denominators, but with the same value, e.g. $\frac{1}{2}$ and $\frac{2}{4}$

even numbers which are exactly divisible by 2

faces any surface of a 3-D solid

factor a whole number which divides exactly into another number, for example the factors of 8 are 1, 2, 4 and 8

fraction expressing one number as a part of another number forms a fraction, for example one out of two is a half (written as $\frac{1}{2}$)

heptagon a polygon that has seven interior angles and seven sides

hexagon a polygon with six sides and six angles

mean the average value of a set of numbers, found by adding up all of the values and dividing by the number of values

median the mid-point of a set of data

minimum the lowest value

mode the most common value in a set of data

multiple a whole number that is the product of another number is one of its multiples

net a series of adjoining 2-D shapes that will fold up together to form a 3-D solid

percentage a proportion when stated out of 100

perimeter the distance around the edge of a 2-D shape

pie chart a circle where sectors are marked with their areas representing the proportion of that part of a group of categories

prime a number that only has two factors, 1 and itself

prism a 3-D solid with two identical faces parallel and joined by parallelograms, which are at right angles to the end faces in a right-angled (right) prism.

quadrilateral a 2-D polygon with four sides and four angles

quarter one-fourth of a whole

radius the length of a straight line from the centre of a circle to the circumference

range the difference between the largest and the smallest value in a set of numbers

rectangle a quadrilateral with opposite pairs of sides parallel and of equal lengths, and all angles right angles

right angle a square angle or corner measuring 90 degrees exactly

rounding the process of approximating a number to a given degree of accuracy, e.g. nearest ten. Where the first number 'dropped off' is 5 or more, the number in the next column is rounded up, e.g. 375 to the nearest ten becomes 380

series (or sequence) a set of numbers where there is a pattern determining the difference between each term of the series

speed the measure of distance travelled in a given amount of time. Its units will have a unit of length per unit of time, e.g. km per hour.

square-based pyramid a 3-D solid with a square base and four triangular faces joining a point

tally chart a method of recording data using short lines, one for each object or count, grouped into fives for easy addition

total the sum of a number of values all added together

triangle a 3-sided polygon with three angles

triangular-based pyramid a 3-D solid with a triangular base and three triangular faces joining a point

vertex (vertices) corners

volume the amount of space within a solid shape

x-**axis** the name given to the horizontal line going across a graph

y-**axis** the name given to the vertical line going along a graph

Answers

Number – Now it's your turn!

1. 26
2. 730
3. 490
4. 88
5. 166
6. 539
7. £3.40
8. £7.01
9. 14.2
10. 658
11. 11
12. 4
13. £16.50
14. **a** 8 bags **b** 7 left over
15. 175,000
16. 76
17–20. 15, 18, 21, 24, 27, 30, 33, 36
 16, 20, 24, 28, 32, 36, 40, 44, 48
 21, 28, 35, 42, 49, 56, 63, 70, 77, 84
 18, 27, 36, 45, 54, 63, 72, 81, 90, 99, 108
21. 14, 35, 56
22. **a** $1 \times 226, 2 \times 113$,
 b $1 \times 165, 3 \times 55, 5 \times 33, 11 \times 15$
 c $1 \times 87, 3 \times 29$
 d $1 \times 144, 2 \times 72, 3 \times 48, 4 \times 36, 6 \times 24$,
 $8 \times 18, 9 \times 16, 12 \times 12$
23. 13, 31, 17
24. 1, 2, 4
25. 22
26. 60
27. 55
28. $1 \times 48, 2 \times 24, 3 \times 16, 4 \times 12, 6 \times 8$
29. **b** 12 **c** 3 **d** 42 **e** 24

30–38. Values:
 100 — one hundred
 2,000,000 — two million
 30 — thirty
 40,000 — forty thousand
 0.5 or $\frac{5}{10}$ — five tenths or one-half
 600,000 — six hundred thousand
 0.07 or $\frac{7}{100}$ — seven hundredths
 8,000 — eight thousand
 9 — nine units or nine ones
39. **a** 8000 **b** 0.08 or $\frac{8}{100}$ **c** 8
 d 800,000
40. **a** 470 **b** 200 **c** 9192 **d** 0 **e** 1,000
41. 793.01, 791.34, 783.84, 758.66, 758.48, 739.93
42. $\frac{8}{12}$ and $\frac{12}{18}$
43. **a** $\frac{2}{3}$ **b** $\frac{7}{10}$ **c** $\frac{4}{5}$
44. 970
45. $\frac{21}{40}$
46. £24
47. £63.75
48. £75
49. £5.61
50. 72
51. £2300 : £1380 : £920
52. **a** £2400, £2000, £1600 **b** £7000
53. 300 g flour, 100 g sugar
54. 7.5 km
55. £44.98
56. £8.40
57. £2.79
58. 21p

Number test

1. $211 + 54 = 265 =$ CCLXV
2. 21, 28
3. 1277
4. 717
5. 6
6. 5020
7. 81, 135, 207
8. 63 and 84
9. *Any two of:*
 a $1 \times 42, 2 \times 21, 3 \times 14, 6 \times 7$
 b $1 \times 35, 5 \times 7$
 c $1 \times 24, 2 \times 12, 3 \times 8, 4 \times 6$
10. **a** 11 **b** 6 **c** 100
11. 0.1053, 0.109, 0.127, 0.129, 0.1309
12. **a** 3000 **b** 10,100 **c** 100 **d** 8900 **e** 3,000,000
13. **a** $\frac{4}{5}$ **b** $4\frac{1}{4}$ **c** $5\frac{1}{9}$ **d** $31\frac{1}{2}$ **e** $\frac{28}{32}$ **f** $\frac{9}{10}$
 g $5\frac{2}{9}$ **h** $\frac{1}{18}$
14. £18.75
15. 80%
16. £340
17. **a** 6 : 4 : 11 **b** 14 : 8 : 5 **c** 1 : 5 : 3
18. 2 cm
19. 3 km
20. 87.15
21. 11.88
22. £15.16
23. £1867.50
24. £44,500

Shape and space – Now it's your turn!

1 **a** $x = 105°$; $y = 24°$;   **b** $x = 25°$; $y = 118°$
2 east
3 **a** 39° **b** 48°   **c** 32°
4 290 sq cm
5 square-based pyramid
6 c and d
7 heptagon
8 84 cm sq
9 96 cm sq
10 684 m
11 2 cans
12 **a** 2400 ml **b** 750 ml **c** 3750 ml
13 3 m
14 14   60
15 **a**   **b**   **c**

16 No lines: F, Z, R, S
    One line: A, W, B
    Two lines: H, X
17 **a** 27 **b** 9   **c** 0
18 120 ml
19 **a** 1.92 m² **b** £548
20
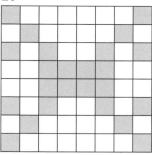

Shape and space test

1 **a** 32 **b** 64   **c** 12
2 **a** 4 m² **b** 14.9 m²
3 8, 16, cone
4 89.5 cm²
5 24
6 **a** kite, 1 **b** parallelogram, 0 **c** pentagon, 5

7 47.6 m³
8 triangular-based pyramid
9 **a** 136 cm² **b** 13 cm²
10 **a** 105 **b** 1428
11 **a** 102 **b** 120 **c** 134

Measure – Now it's your turn!

1 0.95 m/95 cm
2 176 ounces
3 20
4–8

Time in words	12-hour clock	24-hour clock
Half past three in the afternoon	**3:30pm**	**15:30**
Twenty to eleven in the evening	**10:40pm**	**22:40**
Quarter to nine in the morning	**8:45am**	**08:45**
Five past seven in the evening	**7:05pm**	19:05
One minute to midday	11:59am	**11:59**

9 1 hour 15 mins
10 18:03

11 12:31pm
12 43.5 mph
13 40 mins
14 5 metres/second
15 1680 miles
16–23

6:00am	9:00am	12:00 noon	3:00pm	6:00pm
3°C	**5°C**	**9°C**	**10°C**	**6°C**
Change	+ 2°	+4°	+ 1°	–4°

9:00pm	midnight	3:00am	6:00am
2°C	**–1°C**	**–3°C**	**–2°C**
–4°	–3°	–2°	+1°

Measure test

1 **a** 12:15 **b** 14:30 **c** 18:05 **d** 22:18
2 **a** 0.72 litres
    b 5.3 cm
    c 0.053 m
    d 10,000 g
    e 130,000 cm
    f 17030 mm
    g 0.01703 km
    h 1703 cm
3 4560 ml
4 **a** 47 min **b** 38 min **c** 83 min

5 **a** 11:35 **b** 20 min **c** 2h 15 min
    d 25% **e** 50 min
6 **a** 95 miles **b** 135 km **c** 175 miles
7 **a** –3°C **b** 16°C **c** –20°C
8 **a** 40 min
    b 1 h 15 min (75 min)
    c 1 hour
9 **a** 2.4 kg
    b 0.9 litres
    c 85°C
    d 24 jars

Algebra – Now it's your turn!

1 –2
2 1
3 12
4 4
5 11
6 30
7 4
8 a 24   b 6   c 307

Linear sequences – Now it's your turn!

1 51
2 410
3 –9
4 21
5 36
6 126
7 0.91
8 $\frac{5}{10}$
9 61
10 37

Problem solving – Now it's your turn!

1 a 15 seconds   b Ted
2 30
3 £75.20
4 13,790
5 880
6 4
7 10 years
8 1.5 minutes

Data and graphs – Now it's your turn!

1 a 4   b 4   c 3
2 £3.07
3 a 100   b 17   c 10   d 7
4 a Dale   b Guy   c 9
5 a 4   b train   c 14
6 a 75   b $\frac{2}{15}$ c 24%

Algebra, sequences, problem solving and data and graphs test

1 a 13°;   b day 3 & day 4   c day 2   d 9.6°
2 a 7   b 6   c 22   d 7   e 3
3 1 kg (or 1000 g)
4 a 156, 150   b 9, 14   c 6.75, 8.00
   d 13, 21   e 6$\frac{2}{3}$, 5
5 1 year
6 £28.84
7 a F   b F   c F   d F   e T
8 3 letters
9
10 11:20
11 60
12 a 19   b 36   c 72   d 88   e 27.5
13 a coffee   b mint and vanilla   c 60

a 14   b 15   c 11

Non-verbal reasoning – Now it's your turn!

1	c	16	b
2	e	17	d
3	e	18	a
4	d	19	b
5	c	20	d
6	b	21	d
7	d	22	e
8	c	23	d
9	c	24	d
10	a	25	c
11	e	26	e
12	d	27	b
13	c	28	e
14	e	29	d
15	e	30	c

Non-verbal reasoning test

1	d	11	b
2	e	12	e
3	d	13	c
4	e	14	c
5	c	15	d
6	c	16	c
7	e	17	e
8	c	18	a
9	d	19	e
10	c	20	b

Standard CEM Maths and non-verbal reasoning pull-out test

1 46.69   46.92   49.01   62.14   64.69
2 42, 21
3 **a** 217   **b** 522   **c** 3050
4 23.2 cm
5 181 cm
6 **a** 43   **b** 6   **c** 126
7 6 cm
8 9
9 **a** 43   **b** 547   **c** 65
10 6 hours 11 minutes
11

5	7	10
9	12	1
8	3	11

12 **a** isosceles triangle   **b** pentagon
13 **a** $\frac{7}{10}$ **b** $\frac{4}{5}$ **c** $\frac{3}{11}$ **d** $\frac{2}{5}$
14 £300
15 A' (−2,6)   B' (−4,1)   C' (−4,8)   D' (−6,6)
16 128.2 cm
17 **a** 35 m   **b** 86 sq m
18 **a** 10   **b** $\frac{1}{6}$ **c** 30
19 **a** 180 km   **b** 110 km   **c** $\frac{1}{10}$
20 **a** 2280 g   **b** 17.12 kg
21 e
22 e
23 c
24 d
25 d
26 e
27 a
28 c
29 d
30 c
31 c
32 d
33 e
34 c
35 e
36 c
37 a
38 d
39 b
40 e
41 d
42 **a** mango   **b** chocolate
   c vanilla and strawberry   **d** 80
43 **a** 28   **b** 29   **c** Friday
44 **a** Day 5   **b** 4   **c** Day 4 and Day 8   **d** 7   **e** 3
45 **a** 14%   **b** 84%   **c** Yolanda

Resources

www.bond11plus.co.uk

The Bond website is a fantastic resource for all things 11+

For Bond CEM Maths and Non-verbal Reasoning the following books
are recommended:

CEM Maths and Non-verbal Reasoning Assessment Papers 10–11+ years

CEM Maths and Non-verbal Reasoning Assessment Papers 9–10 years

CEM Maths and Non-verbal Reasoning Assessment Papers 8–9 years

Bond CEM-Style Test Papers

For further practice of the subjects covered in this book, the following books
are recommended:

Bond Maths Ten Minute Tests 9–10

Bond Maths Ten Minute Tests 10–11+

Bond Non-verbal Reasoning Ten Minute Tests 9–10

Bond Non-verbal Reasoning Ten Minute Tests 10–11+

CEM How To Do Maths and Non-verbal Reasoning